The Tuesday Blade

a novel by

Bob Ottum

SIMON AND SCHUSTER

NEW YORK

—For G. Safier

one

SHE CAME OUT of the hotel and turned right. The Caddie was parked halfway down the block where he had said it would be, engine running, the tinted windows up. She walked over to it and waited until he leaned across from the driver's seat and unlocked the door, and then, swinging her coat around, she got in. She closed the door and they both looked straight ahead, out the front window. It was 1:15 A.M.

"C'mon," he said. He held his right hand over in front of her chin, the palm up.

"I only have fifty," she said.

The hand stayed there, fingertips slightly curled. The underside of the fingernails extended out a bit from his fingertips. He continued to look ahead; he was slumped down easily, his legs apart. "I thought, you know, I thought for one little second there that you said only fifty," he said.

"That's it. It's slow tonight. Sorry."

"You jive-assing me, blondie. You been gone all day."

"I stopped for dinner."

He snapped his fingers once, then straightened out his hand again. "Come on."

She reached into the front of her blouse where the top three buttons were undone and pulled up the money, folded over, a twenty on top. She put it in his hand and then folded both of her own hands on top of the purse in her lap.

He slipped the bills into his left inside coat pocket without looking at them. "Lady," he said, "you a big fucking disappointment to me."

"I can do better."

"Stopped for dinner. Shee-it."

"No, I can. Really."

"Ain't no way. You wastin' my time."

"Tomorrow."

"Tomorrow, shit. Got to be now, baby. Like, I'm busy. You new to me, like, strange, and I got to put up with this? Three, four hundred I told you and three, four hundred you said."

"This was my first night, though. I mean, since we met, you know."

He took a deep breath, slouching further, knees apart. "You should of done me right. You could get real hurt. Like, messed up bad."

"One more chance. Come on."

He shook his head. "No more chance. Out. Listen— I got a business to run. Folks to see. You assin' me around."

"I'll be here tomorrow," she said. "You'll see."

She half leaned toward him, her purse in both hands. He continued staring ahead. "Tomorrow, shit," he said. "Out."

"Well, then. One more thing."

He yawned. "What?"

She lifted her right hand out of the purse, and when she rolled her wrist over, the blade of the razor folded out and locked. She swung it across his chest quickly and the edge went in just under his left ear. Then, bracing her feet for leverage, she pulled it smoothly across his throat, pressing down, cutting through the left carotid artery first, then into the cartilage of his Adam's apple, finishing the stroke under his right ear, cutting into the right carotid artery.

The line of blood followed along behind the blade, starting in a trickle at first, then spurting—finally surging around from left to right in a sluice. He sucked in his breath and brought both hands up at the same time, fingers apart, and clutched at his throat. He swung his head around to look at her, his eyes widening. He pulled his hands away and looked at them and then put them back to his neck, almost gently. She reached around the headrest with her left hand and sank her fingers into his hair and pulled his head back to open the wound. The blood began pumping out now, cascading down into his gold chains and over the front of his shirt.

She reached across him again with the razor, edge down, and started the next cut just on top of his left thigh. She pulled the blade toward her, bearing down hard at the femoral artery, slicing on across his genitals where his pants were tight, and coming back up to the top of his right thigh. And then she wiped the blade clean on his right kneecap, first this way, then that way, like stropping the razor. She held it up and looked closely at the blade, then flipped it closed. She raised up slightly in the seat and slipped the razor into her right front pocket.

She opened the door and swung her legs around and stepped out. He still had his head back, both hands at his throat, and the blood was spilling out between all his fingers and down the backs of his wrists. She turned and pushed the lock button down again and slammed the door. It was 1:25 A.M.

When she got to Sixth Avenue, she could hear the horn on the Caddie start to blow steadily and, waiting for the light to change, she listened to it over the traffic. He had probably slumped forward to grab at his lap. She pulled her coat around, overlapping it right to left, and tied the belt in a once-over so that the ends would hang just right. It was a cashmere coat, camel-colored.

She walked in under the portico of the Hilton where the cabs circle in, sidestepped around the back of a limousine, then paused until the doorman swung open the door. She smiled at him faintly, nodding. She turned left and walked through the lobby, buttoning up two buttons on the blouse. At the entrance to the Roman Pub she paused again, adjusting her eyes to the light.

"Ma'am?"

"I'm meeting someone, thanks," she said.

Midpoint in the room, Nancy swung around in her chair, waving her drink in one hand and smiling. "Over here," she said.

She walked to the table, untying the coat. "Listen, I'm sorry I'm so late. Really. I honestly thought that I could get away quicker."

Nancy shrugged. "'S all right. You sure didn't miss much. What do you want to drink? A Scotch or something?" She waved for the waitress. "Maybe a martini."

"I don't now. Just something not too strong. Maybe a gin fizz or a . . ."

"A gin *fizz?*"

She nodded at the waitress and sat down. "Well, you know. Something not so strong. But anyway, how did your meeting go?"

Nancy shrugged again. "So how do they all go? I mean, dumb speakers, that dumb panel. Everybody wearing those dumb god-damn batik blouses or whatever. You know."

"Uh huh. Well. You're the one who wanted all this, remember. The sisters all shoulder to shoulder in the movement and all that stuff."

"Mmmm hmmm. So I'm crazy. All right. So I've still got to go to the discussion groups; listen: I belong. And I've still got to look at all those radical broads in their aviator glasses. But still, you got to face up to it. I mean, the feminists are really trying to help. Me. Somebody independent like you, even. You've only been in town . . . what? How many weeks now?"

She waited until the waitress put the drink down and walked away. Then she raised the glass and looked at the pink foam on the top. She took a small sip and put the glass back down on the table. And she leaned back and crossed her right leg over her left, feeling the curve of the razor in her pocket.

"It seems like years already," she said.

two

She had almost always had that look, a sort of cool and stand-away air. It had started taking shape when she had been very small. Her daddy loved it and fostered it. "Glory's got a nifty go-to-hell quality, that one," he would tell the rest of the family. More privately, to his men friends at the school, he would say, "You know, the kid's attitude is strictly kiss-my-ass. And I don't know but what that's not real good with things the way they are these days."

And now she had two bags packed and sitting out on the front porch and there was nothing that anybody could do to stop her because that's the way she was, the way she had always been.

In her father's mind, there was a bigger sin than leaving town. "You've just got a year to go," he said.

"Look, Daddy, I can always go back to school."

"They say it. But they never do it. Never, not once you quit and go."

"Trust me," she said.

"I ought to trust you one right in the seat of the pants, that's what I ought to do."

But he had half smiled and made a face when he said it; they were all in complete surrender now and all the heavy infighting was over. Her mother had finally risen from her bed when she figured out that it wouldn't change anything, and now she was back to painting still lifes, lips all pursed tightly, jabbing at the canvas and ruining the tips of her brushes.

This was on the back porch, which Daddy had fixed up as a

sort of studio, mostly by turning over the washtubs and putting planks across them and then fixing up a homemade easel. Gloria leaned against the doorway and watched.

"You're getting a nice Van Gogh effect that way," she said. "But you're ruining more brushes again. Every time you get mad you do that."

Her mother sniffed. "Who cares? I mean, certainly nobody in THIS family cares. You don't care. Your daddy hasn't got time to care. Your baby brother. Anybody. Van *Go*, even."

"Why do you keep painting those zinnias in wicker pots? Always zinnias. God."

"Don't use the Lord's name like that. Don't you swear around me. Go swear around your fancy New York friends if you want to swear. Your uppity cousin. Besides, I've told you, if you want to learn to paint a still life well, you keep on painting the same still life until you get it *right*. I want to paint these here zinnias; I like them. Well, I've got plenty of zinnias, haven't I? For all you care, I mean."

"Mom."

"Oh, I know, I know. But you're only twenty."

"I've always been something like twenty. I was born twenty. Older, maybe."

"That's your daddy talking again and that's smart-aleck talk. You were born when you were *born* and I ought to know. I was there, wasn't I? Icy-cold girl, indeed. Go-to-heck quality. Huh. You wore crinoline dresses right along with everybody else; it was your father who gave you this here meanish streak."

"Well. Wanting to leave home isn't really mean. It's just . . . well. It's just that everybody leaves home sooner or later. You left . . ."

"Oh, sure. I moved from right over there next door over to this house when your father and I got married. And I respected *my* mother."

She went over and hugged her from behind, hugging up the smell of burnt sienna. Her mother had smelled of oil paints and turpentine for years now; before that, she had smelled of Coty's Emeraude and baked bread. "Come on. Look, we promised not to fight any more, all right? And I'm leaving in about half an hour, soon as Buddy gets back from the school."

"All right, then. I know. Well, go on and check your room one more time. Stuff's thrown all around up there so I'll never get it all straightened around again. Don't know what you're taking and what you're leaving behind. And set out the pie for Buddy when you go through the kitchen. He'll want some pie before you-all leave."

"He's going to turn into a pie, you don't stop feeding it to him."

"If it'll help any to keep him home, I'll give it to him for *break*fast. At least Buddy isn't . . ."

She walked back through the house, letting the voice trail away behind her, and went upstairs and looked at the room again. Just thinking, not talking out loud, she could swear as much as she liked. And Christ on a *crutch*. It was like being in a chintz *blizzard*. Damned pink and red blossomy chintz—drapes and bedspread and pillow covers; ruffles all around the edge of the vanity and even around the vanity *stool*. Her mother had added it a bit at a time, starting years ago, almost as if she was doing it on the sly to force her into a more dainty and ladylike puberty or something. It seemed like every day she had come home from school some new chintz something had been added, all floweredy and crispy, for God's sake. She and her first cousin Nancy had spent hours in here, the door closed, kneeling down with their elbows up on the sill and blowing cigarette smoke out the open window. "Let's see," Nancy would say, looking all around. "We'll get up here tomorrow and Auntie'll be waiting here with your new chintz eyeballs and teeth covers."

She walked in and sat down on the vanity stool and swung it around to look at herself in the mirror.

Down below, she could hear Daddy and Buddy coming in, the screen door slamming behind them, Buddy saying, "All right, where's the Zinnia Queen?" Zinnia Queen, my fanny.

Okay, then. Let's see: first the escape. She would be gone for twenty, maybe even thirty years, and then she would suddenly reappear in town. She'd drive up in a silver Mercedes or something, and she'd be wearing a camel-colored cashmere polo coat, the classic one, the belt all tied carelessly at the waist. And good shoes and a floppy hat and real kidskin gloves, chocolate-colored, with the three stitched lines down the back. It would be like the old television thing of Ingrid Bergman in *The Visit*. She would just flat, suddenly show up and offer to give the town a million dollars. Or maybe even to build a new fine arts center at the school. They would fall all over her. Pictures, interviews. They'd all love her then. And what would she want in return? Maybe put her name on the building? Like, *Gloria Cooper Hall*. No, not really. What she would want was a few old wrongs righted. Revenge. A few heads on platters, things like that. Or maybe make Daddy the president of Greer State J. C.; that's about the only way he'd ever become president of anything. Christ, oh, dear; he'd be the only junior-college president in the country who would go around in an Athletic Department gray sweat shirt with his coach's whistle hanging around his neck on the black twine. When she had been very small, she had asked Daddy if he wore the whistle to bed over his jammies, and he had laughed a lot and looked at Mother across the table. "Hell-fire, I might as well," he had said, and Mother had gotten up from the table and left the room. It wasn't too long after that that she had started painting still lifes.

Well, hell. She leaned forward and looked at herself more closely, checking all across the top of her nose for blemishes.

She suspected, no, wait, she *counted* on, being a whole lot better looking than she thought she was. You could tell when men turned and looked at you on the sidewalk, or when they stared at your chest in class. But then you'd rush home and look in the mirror and wonder what it was that they thought they had seen. Buddy had told her that the world was divided pretty much in half: some men were ass men and some men were tit men. Well. Okay, her rear end was probably too slim and boyish, all right. But she did have nice boobs; Lord, everybody in town knew that. Especially in the week before her period. And she could pass the pencil test that she had read about in—where?—uhhh, *Cosmopolitan* or something. Put a pencil under one breast and then let it go. If the pencil fell out, fine. If it stayed tucked up under your breast, you couldn't go around without wearing a brassiere; too flopsy. Well, when she got to New York, where nobody had ever seen her, she was going to try going around without a bra. Nancy probably did. Hell, by now Nancy probably went around without any *pants* on.

Everything else was pretty standard. She knew that she was too tall to ever make any cute moves. She was too square-shouldered and she knew that she was too strong, but she had really liked being strong as a kid and she was stuck with it now. "A little weight training never hurt anybody, and especially a kid with a temper like Glory," Daddy had said, but finally the girls' gym teacher had made her stop lifting weights when she was eleven and had started developing tiny biceps, for God's sake. She had gone on to field hockey, where she could clobber everybody with the stick and pretend that it was by accident. And temper; Lord, that had been years ago, when she had been really small. She used to get riled a lot, that's all. If she was playing outfield and missed an easy pop fly, she would chase the ball across the grass and then grab it up and shake it and bite it really hard a few times before throwing it back.

"Glory?" It was Buddy from down below. "Come on. We got to go here."

Glory: the name had started out as Gloria. Gloria-Ann Cooper, in fact, but in the soft, whipped-divinity accents of Greer County, Oklahoma, in just the right wind, Gloria sounded just like Glory and it had stayed that way. When she had been younger, she and Nancy had changed their names a lot. Nancy was three years older and read more stuff and got to all the better names first, all the longer ones full of syllables. Then Gloria had finally settled on Stormy, which was perfect and sounded just like somebody with ice-blue eyes, and she tried to get everybody to call her Stormy, but nobody would. But it was all right; everything in her diary was signed that way the last year she had kept it, and now it read just like another girl had come up to the room and written in all the secrets.

She looked at her nose again. The honest Cooper nose, which was way too honest as far as she was concerned. She sure as hell would have preferred more of a dishonest little old nose, like maybe Annette Funicello's, but there you go. It was all she had and it came with the body, with the gray eyes and the good teeth with the slight family overbite, and the full, pouty mouth that she had made damned sure was a full, pouty mouth by pooching out her lips all the time until it became a habit.

"Listen, you comin' or not?"

"Yes, yes. Just hold on," she said.

Hold your ass, dummy; there was plenty of time yet.

Well, all right. He *was* still a sort of damn dummy, even if he was getting better. He had almost always been bigger than she was, even though he was a year younger, but she had been the one who had to go around doing *his* fighting. There was still a tiny scar right at the corner of her lower lip. That was from the gang bang, which only Buddy knew about.

Well, okay. It was a rape, really. Luis Rodriguez, that Messkin, had gotten her into his barn and then into the back seat of his dad's old black Pontiac. They had been playing Apache and he had her hands all tied behind her as a captive cowboy. And he had hit her in the mouth hard a couple of times until she had begun bleeding around the gums and everything, and he had pulled off her Levi's and then her dirty cotton underpants. She was ten years old and Luis was thirteen.

Then he had tied clothesline around her ankles, which had really burned, and he had tied one of her ankles to one door handle and the other ankle to the handle on the other side, opening her legs wide.

"You holler, I'm really gonna hit you," he had said—and then he had unbuttoned his pants and taken it out. It was the first erect penis she had ever seen; she had seen Buddy's limp little thing plenty of times when he had been getting ready for bed or something like that. And there had been one calm little corner of her mind that allowed as how this one really didn't look all that bad. It looked a little bit like a brownish torpedo, or a rocket ship, maybe; all smooth and a little bit curved up, with that slit eye at the end of it like a tiny window. But then he had scrunched way down in between her legs, bracing his knees up against the back seat, and had shoved it up into her, pumping hard again and again, and it had hurt to beat hell, the pain all hot and dry. And she had gone pretty crazy, biting out at the air so that he had to arch his shoulders way back to keep away from her teeth.

When he had finished and taken it out, the rocket ship had been still stiff but there had been blood flecked all around the sides of it; he had put it back into his pants and then looked down at her crotch. "Shee-it," he had said. "You ain't even got any hairs on there." And then he had climbed over the front seat and gone out the door on the driver's side.

She had still been crying when she had heard them in the barn; he had come back with some of the other Messkins, standing just outside the Pontiac. "Five cents and you kin fuck her," he had said. "Come on. Nickel apiece, you guys. It's really good stuff and, boy, she likes it. I'm not foolin'."

And, one by one, they had climbed in and done it to her, four kids from school with their stiff little penises like stinging torpedoes. But when Luis had gone out to try to get more customers, nobody else had any nickels, and he had finally come back and untied her. She had been too tired to move fast, so all she could do was lie there and look up at him.

"You want some more?" he had said. "Want me to do it to you again?"

She had shaken her head no. There was crusted blood around her lips.

"Then go on home. You say anything to any*body* and I'll kick the livin' shit out of you, you hear?"

She had heard. In fact, she had told only Buddy about it and, right off, he had been too scared to do anything. "Jeez, Glory," he had whined, "those big guys'll kill me."

She had slept for almost two days, and when she had gotten up, she had put on her coveralls and gone down to the Athletic Department at the school. Her daddy had been out on the field, coaching the freshman football squad. She had gone into Daddy's equipment room and gotten his pool cue. It was his special pride; it screwed apart in the middle into two pieces and the handle part had little diamond-shaped mother-of-pearl insets inlaid in the swirly pecan wood. She had taken the bottom half and left.

It had taken another four days to get him. Ahhh, Luis, you bad-ass bugger. She had waited and waited down by the creek where all the Messkin kids swam and, finally, he had come ambling down the path.

"Hey, Luis," she had said. She had planted both feet wide in the correct big-league stance that Daddy had taught her, overlapping her grip, and when he had looked up, she had swung the pool cue hard like a baseball bat. The first shot had broken his nose and his right cheekbone and the eyetooth on that side. And when he brought his hands up to his face, she had cocked the cue and swung it again, shattering all the knuckles on his left hand.

Luis never told anybody about it and Glory didn't either. When he graduated from high school, his face was still all crooked.

But hell-fire. Everybody has a bad part like that sooner or later in life. Everybody has something, and a lot of people have a lot worse things to worry about than gang bangs. She figured she was lucky to get away with just the tiny scar on her mouth. Anyway, she had gotten even and that settled that.

Mostly, her life was all put together. She had been jumpy around boys for a year or so when she had gotten bigger and her breasts and things had come out—she had the biggest, earliest boobs in her class for a long time—but you couldn't go around being jumpy all the time. And by her freshman year at Greer, she was letting selected boys feel them, and she was feeling the selected boys right back. Feeling down there, too, until they would both be shuddering and sort of nibbling at each other's necks and generally fogging up all the windows on the car. Once they got her skirt up around her waist, she would let her legs be eased apart slowly and it was strange and wonderful how a boy's hand could fit perfectly down in there, the palm down and all his fingers bunched together like that, his thumb pressing into the side of her thigh. But she would stop it right there every time, just when they would gently slide the hand back up so that they could hook their thumb under the elastic waistband of her panties to get down inside. Not now. Uh uh. Outside, yes. But not inside. No Way.

She wondered if Nancy was letting guys do it to her in New York. There was no indication in her letters, but then, you couldn't write about stuff like that in letters anyway, where somebody else might read it. Anybody who would sneak chintz into a room would read letters. She'd ask Nancy about it when she got there to the apartment and Nancy would sure enough tell her. In fact, she would even, when the right time came, let the right guy get his hand down inside there, really underneath the pants this time. Well. Well, provided that he was six-four or so; a big Scandinavian with really broad shoulders and a flat stomach and a lot of hair on his chest and had maybe a reddish fluffy beard and he smelled sort of like canvas or cracked leather, and every single tooth was perfect and he had heavy eyebrows, also reddish. And money and a Datsun Z-28. Otherwise, no. Well. And provided that she just happened to be wearing really pretty panties at the time. You know.

When she came back to town in the cashmere coat, when she was a success, maybe she would bring the big Scandinavian with her so that everybody could see what she meant.

Buddy was at the door now. "Goddamn, Glory," he said. "You know how *long* it takes to drive to Oklahoma City?"

She stood and looked around the room for the last time. "Okay," she said. "Okay, I'm all set. Let's go."

He looked around, too. "God dog. Boy, I'd go off to New York, too. Anyplace, get away from this screwy room. What is all this stuff again?"

"It's called chintz," she said.

three ▬▬▬▬▬▬▬▬▬

CHRIST's *sake*. They were nothing if not obvious. This one walked right up to her, snapping his fingers on both hands, and stood right there all loose and jangly, his pelvis thrust forward. He said, "Wha's happenin', baby?"

She couldn't understand him at first, the whole accent was so silky. "Mmmmmm?"

"Like, wha's happenin'? You need any help?"

She shook her head no. "Nothing is happening. And no, I don't need any help at all."

He nodded, seeming to accept that. But he didn't go away. "Somebody din' meet you, sugah. Tha's right?"

Lord, Lord. She put both bags down on the floor and stood up straight again. "Well," she said, "let me put it this way: Get away from me, you son of a bitch."

They looked into each other's eyes for a long second and finally he nodded. "Dig," he said. And he walked away, still snapping his fingers.

Ye gods. It had taken her some time, almost an hour now, to figure out that Nancy wasn't there. Well, at least not if she had all this figured out correctly. She had gotten off the airport bus from Newark and picked up her bags and had gone right down to the main concourse of the terminal. Port Authority, all right—but it was an awful lot bigger than she had thought it would be. There were bus ramps even going overhead and various departure gates all around and people all pushing. She had waited near the gate for a while, right where she had come out, looking into passing faces, her stomach starting to growl. Then she had walked over a few feet to stand in front of the Hoffritz cutlery shop window. But, no. And she had picked up both her bags and gone down to the main level and out in front. She looked up and down Ninth Avenue for a few minutes. And finally she had gone back up to the concourse and back over to the gate. She was starving.

The other thing had started right away, practically the first time she put her bags down on the floor. It must be something about standing still and looking puzzled in the Port Authority Terminal. And being alone.

It worked roughly like this: The man would come by in one direction, strolling more slowly than anybody else, and glance over at her. Sometimes she would notice him, sometimes not. But she would sure enough notice him when he came back again going in the other direction.

All of them paused, missing maybe just a beat in their step, looking directly at her and raising their eyebrows ever so slightly. If she looked away, most of them walked on. She was not used to looking away from anybody and she didn't like it— but it's a stunt you can learn in the first two minutes in New York City, for God's sake. Some of them came right up, cool and smiling. And every damn single one of them was wearing some kind of gold-chain necklace or a medallion, their shirts open down to here. Holy smokes. They would ask her if she needed any help and she would tell them to go stick it in their goddamn ear.

No, no, she wasn't lost. No, she didn't need any help. Yes, she knew where to go. No, she *lived* here. Beat it.

All right, all right. Feeling undressed is one thing; you can feel just about as undressed back home by any Oklahoma hayshaker as anybody. The town probably doesn't matter. But now she felt, well, she felt like some sort of *crotch* display in a department store window or something, almost as if the front of her slacks were transparent and everybody could look right into some little window right at it. She folded her hands in front, spreading her fingers out. Her stomach hurt.

"You all right?" This one was a cop.

"Mmmm hmmm, thanks. Uh, wait. Where can I find a telephone?"

"Right over there," he said. "And listen, keep an eye on your bags, all right?"

She dialed the number and it rang and rang. Finally, the main switchboard operator came on and said, "Exactly whom are you calling, please?" and she said, "Nancy, uh, Nancy Cavanaugh at *Time* magazine," and the operator said, "Well, there doesn't seem to be any answer there," and she said, "Would you try it maybe one more time, please?" And it rang about eleven more times. And finally somebody answered.

"Nancy Cavanaugh's desk."

About time. "This is Gloria Cooper," she said. "Could I speak to Miss Cavanaugh, please?"

"Glory?"

"Gloria. Cooper. Glor . . . ee . . . *ah*."

"May I ask what this is in reference to, please?"

"Uh, well, I just arrived from out of town—I'm at the Port Authority Bus Terminal—and Nancy was supposed to meet me here. Except that she isn't here."

"She was expecting you?"

"Uh huh."

"Today?"

"Right now, uh huh."

"Hang on just a second."

There was a hand-over-the-mouthpiece, sort of muffled conversation and then a new voice came on.

"Who is this?"

Christ on a *crutch*. "It's Gloria *Cooper*," she said. "I'm Nancy's *cousin*. She's expecting me. She's *been* expecting me. And I'm here. But Nancy—"

"I know," the voice said. "She's not there, right?"

"That's *right*."

"Well, uh, look, one more second, okay?"

And then Voice Number One came back on.

"All right," the girl said. "It's like this. We're all a little upset here, so forgive us. But Nancy was mugged last night. She hadn't said anything about expecting anyone coming in and—"

"Mugged?"

"And robbed. A purse thing. The guy hit her a lot and . . . you know. She's in the hospital."

Her stomach tightened and she half swung around and looked out at the terminal. "Will she be—"

"Oh, yes. I mean, she'll be all *right*. But—"

"What hospital?"

"Harkness Pavilion. We had her moved this morning, our medical. Where are you?"

"Port Authority."

"Oh, God. Well, look, you know where the cabs are?"

"Yes. I went down there once already."

"Well, uh, Gloria, look, maybe you'd just better take a cab and come on up here. I mean, the Time and Life Building on the corner of Sixth and Fiftieth. All right? Sixth Avenue and Fiftieth. They make you stop at reception and they give you a pass to come on up. And we'll think of some—"

She shook her head. "No. No, listen, thank you-all very much. I mean, you're very kind and all. But I'll be fine. The—uh—the Harkness—what?"

"Pavilion. You sure?"

"Yes. And thanks."

"Well, be careful."

Lord, Lord, *Lord*. She tugged in hard on the handle and got the booth door open and looked out at the concourse. The policeman was standing almost directly across from her and she nodded at him. Welcome to Manhattan. Good God.

The phone books were on a rack just off to the side; there were sort of shiny aluminum-like book covers, and they swung up on swivels so that the books could be opened. There were more phone books for just one town than she had ever seen. But all right: Yellow Pages. Look under HOTELS first. And we'll get that part done and then we'll get this damned other mess all straightened out with Nancy. She didn't know any of the hotel names, so she'd have to go for one she figured that she could trust. Holiday Inn, maybe. Or even a Howard Johnson's, if they had . . .

Christ, oh, *dear*. Now what?

It happened like a flash impression and her mind kind of photographed it as it went along. He had come sailing along, head up and looking far across the concourse. A take-out cup in his hand. It had "Savarin" printed on it in fancy letters running up and down the long way, and a Lipton tea label had been fluttering on its string. He was tall. Very, no . . . he was *really* skinny. He had blondish hair, all a mass of curls. Some of the curls were champagne-colored; most of them were beige. There were a few caramel ones in there, too. Blue eyes and a gray glen-plaid suit, exactly the kind of suit that Steve McQueen wore in *The Thomas Crown Affair*.

But now he was all sprawled out, taking up a whole lot of space, and her suitcases were lying on their sides and the tea was splashed way out in front of him, with the teabag sitting like a tiny brown island in the middle of the puddle. It took him a little while to roll over and sit up. And then he crossed his legs and looked up at her.

"How many times do I have to tell you that isn't funny?" he said.

"Oh, uh . . . Well, my bags . . ." She reached down for him.

"Ah, ah. Don't *touch* me," he said. "I'll get up and kick over the phone booth myself, all right?"

"Look, I mean, I'm really sorry. Are you hurt?"

Bluer than Paul Newman's, almost, she thought. Although she remembered that she had read someplace that Paul Newman put trick drops in his eyes to pump up the color.

He shook his head, still sitting. "No. Not hurt. A bit bruised, yes." Then he paused. "Wait a minute. Hear that? Your stomach is growling something awful. That sort of thing is not considered at all chic in New York."

"Well . . . well, I flat can't *help* it."

He looked at the tags on the suitcase handles. "Ummm, E W R," he said. "That stands for Newark in airlinese. An awful place."

"Well, New York CITY isn't just a whole lot to sing and dance about. So far."

"Please," he said. And he got up, more or less in sections, patting carefully at his knees and elbows. "Please. If it's all the same, no personal problems. I'd rather not hear about it." He held up one hand, the palm toward her. "I know already. Your name is Sally Lou Mary Ann Brampson and you're just this very minute in from Lute Song, Minnesota, and Aunt Hattie and Uncle Al aren't here to meet you. And already sixteen rather fey-looking men have approached you with positively *sinful* things on their minds. And now you're sore wrought and your stomach is rumbling. There it goes again. Hear it?"

She nodded. "Never mind my stomach. And anyway, it isn't Minnesota. It's Okla—"

"Whatever." He shrugged. "Now, then. Is it all right if I go now, Sally Lou Mary Ann? You're really cutting into my tea-time."

"Gloria," she said.

"Again?"

She repeated it.

"Not Glory?"

"No."

"Too bad," he said. "Well then."

"Look, I'm sorry about my suitcases and all. I mean, you stumbling like that, and—"

"Oh, no. Please, my dear. I do this all the time. Why, there isn't a *day* that I don't walk across this very terminal and fall down over suitcases or at least somebody's Lhasa apso. All right? But now, I fear, we must part. And let me remember you always like this."

"Okay. Bye. And thanks for being so nice about it all."

"Bye, Glory."

But he walked exactly fifteen steps and then he turned and came back.

"You know, you really do look pretty bad," he said. "Well, I don't mean *bad* bad. I mean worn. Would you care to join me for some tea? Look, we'll get four cups, two for drinking and two for spilling."

"Oh, no, you don't," she said.

He held up the hand again. "Wait. Hold it. When I say *join* me, I don't mean join me *some*where. You can join me right here at the old phone booth, right where we always meet. We'll drink our tea and we'll look at all the funny people passing by. We can even set out your suitcases as a trap, if you'd like."

"Oh. Oh, well . . . uh, look, I'm sorry. I'm not usually this suspicious. It's just that, well. I'm nervous, I guess. And everything—"

"Be right back," he said.

"Well . . . okay. And anyway, long as you're going, maybe you could bring back some kind of munchie, too," she said. "You know. A sweet roll or something. I don't care. Something."

She stood the bags back up, a little more out of the way.

He came back out of the crowd with a cup in each hand and put them down on the satiny sort of aluminum top of the telephone-book counter. "One for you," he said, "and one for me. The doughnut's in my inside coat pocket. Just a second." And he pried off the lids and dropped them on the floor and nudged them under the counter with one foot. "Now, the idea is this: If you want dark tea, you hold this little tag gently like this. Are you with me? And you slosh the tea bag up and down for perhaps thirty-five minutes or so. For light tea, you just dunk it once or twice."

"We have tea in Oklahoma."

"Well, one never knows. I thought perhaps Oklahomans just drank *Indians* or something of that sort. Anyway, I'm sure that you can't have doughnuts like this in old Sleepy Eye. This very doughnut has been aging since—"

"Greer," she said. "It's Greer. The home of Greer State Junior College. My dad is the athletic director there. And, yes. I want it strong. I'm about to flat fall right over."

"Well, drink it slowly now. And when Aunt Hattie and Uncle Al finally get here to meet you, you can introduce me as Mr. Samaritan. Honestly, that is an *awful*-looking doughnut."

She swallowed a big gulp of the tea and then pooched the bite of doughnut over into one side of her cheek so that she could talk. "Well, there isn't an Aunt Hattie or Uncle . . . whatever. There *is* my first cousin Nancy, but she . . . well . . ."

"Happens to everyone," he said.

They sipped at the tea for a few minutes, looking at each other.

"You know," he said, "I don't want this to make you giddy or anything like that. Whatever you do, please don't blush. But I must say, you really are some kind of fine-looking lady."

"I haven't blushed ever in my life. Ever."

"Not *stunning*, mind you. Merely super. Willowy, even."

"You sure have curly hair for a man. There are some—mmm—caramel-looking ones in there."

"I know. I send away for them. All right, then. Finish your tea and I must go."

She put the empty cup down, blinking.

"Tell me about Cousin Nancy."

She shrugged. "She's my cousin, all right. Uh, yes, she is. And she used to call me Stormy. Supposed to meet . . . Ummm, listen, you think I look like a girl whose name is Stormy?"

"Not now," he said.

"Meet me here. She was supposed to, I mean. Meet me. But

she was . . . she got . . . well . . . Oh, you know." She sighed, short of breath.

"Happens to everyone."

"And I called. They told me. Her office, I mean. But nobody gets my first name right. All along, see? You know."

"Right. It's Glory."

She blinked some more, trying to focus on him. "Right. It's just like you said."

"Now, then. Here's the plan," he said. "You take this smaller bag, all right? That's the girl. And I'll carry the bigger one. And you hold onto my arm right here. You know, you're very strong."

"We don't have any ex . . . any escalators in Greer."

"Here. This is my car."

"Oh, no you don't," she said.

"Now look, pay attention now, Glory. I'll just drop you off and then I've really got to dash."

"That's better. All right, then. Because I'm really very strong for a girl."

He closed the door, walked around to the other side and got in. She was already dozing, head back.

"You know, you're right," he said. "You are strong. Your only problem is that you're not very fucking bright."

four

GOD, she *loved* it. It was such a pretty nightie, all sort of really clingy, with all this lacy handwork across the bodice, and she liked to lie there, looking up at the ceiling, feeling the material with just the very tips of her fingers, reading every tiny wrinkle like Braille across her stomach. The ceiling was gold and white, curly gilded things all along the edges, and there was a gold cherub in each corner, looking down at her lying there in her nightie. She loved it. She didn't try to hide from them. The cherubs loved it.

And she slept more than she really wanted; she slept, and each time she awoke, she felt the nightie some more, yawning.

No, wait. This one was a diff— No, *really* wait. Just a minute here. Don't go away again. This was a different nightgown. Different here, across the front. But it felt just as nice, even if Mother wouldn't approve. Daddy probably would. If she had his whistle right now, it would fall right in here between her breasts; probably cold. Cold whistle. So she winked at all the cherubs, all four of them, turning her head to do it. But all that movement made her dizzy and she slept again.

Then: "Drink this," he said.

"No."

"My dear," he said, "I must say, you have the constitution of a *horse*. I've never seen anything like it. Come on now. Please drink it."

"What?"

"Mmmm. Well, it's Campbell's Cream of Tomato Soup. More

or less. There now. That's better, see? And may I suggest that you stop feeling your nightgown that way."

"Sleepy."

"Of *course* you're sleepy. Darling, old Native Dancer would be *dead*. Now, here."

She took a couple more sips so that he would go away. And when he was gone, she slept. And while she was sleeping, one of the cherubs came down off his corner of the ceiling and pushed up her nightie and fucked her. His breath smelled bad. But she let him do it to her anyway because she had to get back to sleep.

No, no. Wait a minute. Easy. Where is everybody? Where is . . . you know, what's her name? Nancy whatever. Besides, this was a new nightie again. God, she *loved* that feel.

Then: "You really must get up now," he said. "It's cleanup time. Brush your teeth and take a nice hot bath. Lots of pink bubbles. Wouldn't you like a bath? After all, cleanliness is next to godliness. Which is why Saturday night is next to Sunday. I just made up that last part right now."

The nightie was gone and she was naked in the bed.

"No."

"Yes, you will. Of course you will."

"No."

But then a nice lady came to help, which was kind of her. And the nice lady stayed right there while she soaked in the tub, the lady kneeling there on the bath mat and saying, "My, such a big, pretty girl," and helping her scrub everything. And then she helped dry her off with a big, fluffy pink towel, using a lot of patting.

"Do you mind if I throw up?" Gloria said.

"Not at all, honey," the nice lady said. And she helped while Gloria knelt down on the thick carpet and hugged both arms around the toilet bowl and threw up. Then Gloria got up and brushed her teeth while the nice lady held her around the waist. And she went back into the bedroom and got into bed.

"Now, sleep," the lady said.

But she woke up again. Easy, now. Just . . . just hold on here. Hello? Anybody? Nancy? Daddy? Wait, breathe deeply one more time. Big ins and outs. Now more. That's it. Listen, there is something bad-awful *wrong* around here, and what you have to do is to get it straight, is what you have to do. You're in trouble. Come on, think. Remember now, like Daddy said: Get your blood going; stir it up, kiddo, and it goes all around your body waking things up. Hello, kidneys. Shake it, kid. It's like . . . No, you don't. Stay awake now and listen to me. Don't sleep. It's like, well, say it's like isometrics, and if you can do a tough word like that inside your head, you're going to be all right here sooner or later. Iso*metrics*. You stretch and then you push your muscles against one another to set up a strain until you shake a lot. Uh huh. Put your palms together and push hard and then breathe hard at the same time. Got it? You got to get this stuff out of your system.

She did maybe fifteen minutes of flexing and pushing, chasing her blood all around, like Daddy said. She napped just a few minutes. And then she did another ten minutes of the isometrics, taking in all the air she could hold. The cherubs watched her from their corners. Those fucking cherubs.

And this time when he came back, she kept her eyes half-closed and went back to the shallow breathing.

He leaned over and stroked her hair. "Feel better now?"

She nodded.

"I knew you would. Health will triumph over all. Now, listen to me, all right?"

Nod.

"You're going to a party tonight. How about that? Well, to be perfectly accurate about this, not *going* to a party. Actually, the party is right here. We have a great many parties right here. Fun, *affectionate* parties. Hmmm? And after the party, a very, very nice man is going to come back here in this room with you. A dear, dear man. Got that part?"

Nod. Easy, now.

"And, of course, you will treat the man very nice."

Uh huh. That's it. And I thought it was the cherub.

"Now, then. We'll bring you in a little dinner in a minute and then someone will come in and make you look all nice again. You'd like that, wouldn't you? *Wouldn't* you?"

All right, all right, damn it. Nod.

"Okay, then." He patted her on the forehead and then gently tugged the front of her nightgown around to cover the nipple of her right breast. "My, my, that's a lovely thing," he said. "You know, you have what is loosely known as a *voluptuous* body. The fountain of all womanhood. An Earth Mother body. Men will crave you whenever they see you from now on. Entire empires will totter and fall. Well, at least this section of Park Avenue. And fortunes will be lavished on your favors. Isn't that something?"

She nodded again.

After he left, she closed her hands into fists and rolled them clockwise until her wrists and forearms hurt. Then she tightened and loosened her shoulders and thighs and abdomen, breathing hard, clenching her teeth until the sides of her jaws hurt bad. Don't sleep now, not again. Come *on*. Do the leg muscles again. *Work*. Clear your head, dummy. Breathe in. *In*, for Christ's sake. There. Okay. How do you feel now? All right, I'll tell you how I feel: that son of a BITCH. Nobody does me this way. That rotten *bastard*. Nobody. Son of a bitch. That's how I feel.

"There now, time to wake up. You want a little soup? And there's a little chop here, too." It was the nice lady again.

Fuck you, too, nice lady. And your chop.

"Just some soup, please."

"There, see? I knew you would feel better, Glory. You've really been sleeping way too much. Now, here."

"Could I go to the bathroom first?"

"Need any help?"

"I don't think so. Not this time. I feel better, really."

"Fine, dear. You go right ahead."

She closed the door and looked around. That son of a bitch will get his. Let's see. Fluffy towels with monograms. More gilt ceiling. She opened the medicine chest. Nothing. Well, aspirin. Some Band-Aids, but they were in a cardboard box and that wouldn't help. A black flat leather case with a snap cover and initials stamped in gold. No. Some Listerine, family size. Gillette Foamy. A tube of Crest. Little electric Schick. Damn, damn. A thing of Brazzi face bronzer. Christ, oh, dear. Some Revlon—what? Charlie. Hmmm. Gillette: the Dry Look. Tube of Vaseline. God*damn* it.

She picked up the leather case again and unsnapped it. The inside was lined in black brushed velvet, all soft.

There were seven straight-edge razors in there, all in a row. Each razor was closed and fitted into its curved velvet slot. The handles were eggshell-white pearl, all soft shine, and the days of the week were hand-lettered on each razor in flowing black, a sort of Gay Nineties script. Sunday. Monday. Tuesday. Wednesday. Thursday. Friday. Saturday.

"Are you all right in there, dear?"

She reached over and flushed the toilet. And then she quickly ran her fingertips down the line of razors. All right, the third up from the bottom. She lifted out the Tuesday razor and snapped the leather case closed.

"Fine," she said. "I'm fine. Be out in just a second."

How? Oh. That was the way they worked. She remembered now that she had seen Daddy do it when she was little; she would sit there on the edge of the tub and watch him lather up and shave with long, careful strokes, each stroke trailing pinkish, clean skin behind it. You hold it in your hand, fitted into the palm, like this. And then you turn your hand over and the blade swings out and around. And it seems to lock into position like that. Well, if you hold your hand just right, the blade stays open. Uh huh. Just like that. She did it a few times, rolling her hand over. Over and back. Open and closed. She reached over and closed the medicine chest.

And she opened the bathroom door and walked out, palming the razor, half behind her, and got back into bed.

"Maybe not the soup after all," she said. "Just a bite of that chop instead."

It turned out to be a sure-enough party, like he had said, even if most of the people went around looking all frosted-eyed, like in *Village of the Damned*. And the lady had helped her look really nice, like he had said, too. Well, if you really like red velveteen gowns cut all the way down to here, for God's sake. Mostly, she stood beside the bar and watched them all, holding her face set just right.

And then the very, very nice man came into the bedroom with her, like he had said, and the very nice man slowly and carefully took off his very nice clothes, hanging everything over the back of the wing chair, pausing to make sure the sleeves were straight. He took off his pants, kicking at the legs just so, and then sat down and pulled off his executive-length socks with the up-and-down elastic ribbing. Finally, he stood and pulled down his very nice boxer shorts with the little pattern printed all over showing pictures of bulls and bears. The mark of the gathered waistband of his shorts still showed across the front of his stomach. He climbed into the bed and got her legs opened just right, carefully lifting up her knees and positioning himself in between them. And then he got hunched over and fucked her, while she held tight to the closed razor up under her pillow, both arms behind her head. The very nice man didn't know that she was holding onto the razor or the very nice man wouldn't have climaxed so quickly inside her.

He dozed for a few minutes, his arms out wide, lying heavily with the top of his head fitted up under her chin. She could smell whiskey and smoke each time he breathed out. Otherwise, there was no feeling at all, only when she tightened and loosened her thigh muscles, working them some more. She looked up at the ceiling and waited, blinking, following the gilded pattern with her eyes.

Then he sighed a little and pushed himself up. He backed out from between her knees and got off the bed and went into the bathroom. She could hear the water running. When he came out to dress, he allowed as how she was really just a wonderful, sweet girl to do this for him. And he would, yes, he really would, leave a little something extra for her when he left. She nodded at him, still lying on her back, both hands behind her head, tucked under the pillow.

She got up and showered, taking the razor into the shower with her, and then got back into bed.

And finally, he came in, all champagne-curly and a little drunk. He sat down on the edge of the bed.

"Sleepy?" he said.

"Not very."

"The nice man said you were very good. Terrific. You were warm and lusty, he said."

"Ummm hmmm."

"If the truth were known, you like it, don't you?"

She nodded.

"Let me hear you say it."

All right. Easy. Be patient, now. "I like it."

He untied his tie and pulled it around and threw it into the chair, then unbuttoned his shirt. "Ah, my dear, it does my heart good to hear you speak so lucidly. I knew you'd come around. Well, you'll forgive that little metaphorical allusion, *come* around. But a big, husky creature like you *has* to like it. It's God's will, and all that. The scheme of things. You know, that wide, honest pelvis and those majestic, gently swaying breasts. A body like yours was specifically *designed* for the act of love, if you follow me. You're going to be great, best in the world. No.

No, more than that, even. You'll be marvelous. We'll be a *team*. I get to be captain, of course. You must forgive my *recruiting* methods; one does what one has to do. You can understand that, I can tell. You stood out in that terminal like Joan of Arc. And, of course, the terminal has always worked for me. And—"

Joan of Arc was *little*, you son-of-a-bitch bugger. But just keep talking. And don't go away now. It's just about time for you.

"—you understand now about the parties. And the *gifts* that accompany the parties. We'll be wonderful. I'll be the host; you'll be the hostess. That's my *role* in life: bringing people together so that they can enjoy—ummm—the company. Lord knows, it's a little enough thing I do, being a social catalyst like this. But it's important in its own humble way. There are so many *lonely* souls out there. And many of them aren't merely lonely—they're *richly* lonely. Generously lonely."

He put his hand down softly on her stomach.

"Listen," he said. "Hear how quiet? The guests have all gone. So much for tonight. Hear? Everybody's gone."

"Except you," she said.

"Except me."

She pulled her left hand out from under the pillow and patted the bed beside her. "You can get on in here if you'd like." Come on, cherub. Come on, you pimp asshole.

"You're not sleepy, you say."

"Not at all."

"Did you have any of the—uh—the soup for dinner?"

"Uh huh, yes. Every drop of it."

"Well, that's good. Listen, are you really all that good?" he said. "I mean, America's sweetheart, like the nice man said?"

"I'm better," she said. She patted the bed again.

He stood up and started taking off his clothes, weaving a bit, looking down at her. He undid his cuff links and dropped them on the floor, then pulled the shirt off over the top of his head, messing the curls around even more. He kicked his pants away to one side.

She watched him, lying quiet. He really had a nice body, strong thighs and a tight, flat stomach, with the ribs rippling up like ladders along each side, and a line of curly, tawny hair running up above his belly button. He pulled down his Jockey shorts and stepped out of them and then stood up straight beside the bed and held out both arms like a circus aerialist seeking applause.

"Tah dah!" he said.

She opened her legs far apart under the covers and braced both heels against the mattress. And under the pillow, she opened the razor.

"Now, really. Ain't I something?"

"You're *something*, all right," she said. She got the blade just right.

He came in closer, his knees pressed against the side of the bed, his back arched and his half-erection hanging just above her face. "You may touch it, my dear," he said. "Just by way of saying hello."

She reached up and touched it gently with her left hand, running the tips of her fingers just under the glans penis where the skin tucked up under like a little plow.

"That's the spot," he said. He closed his eyes.

Then she whipped her right arm around, the open blade shining in the light, and slashed at him, the force of the slice tracing a thin white line all the way down through one testicle. And then, coming up to her knees, she braced her legs wide apart and swung her arm around in a backswing.

There was a sudden burst of blood and urine and it splashed across her stomach and the fronts of her thighs.

He sucked in a big gulp of breath. His arms went wide, fingers apart, and then he brought them back like claws, reaching for her hair. But by now she was arcing fast off the backstroke, rolling her hand over. The blade hit him in the soft roll of fat just above the left hipbone and she pulled it down diagonally across his lower abdomen, bearing down hard, and everything came spilling out behind it.

He opened his mouth again, looking down at her, but no sounds came out.

She looked up at him and they both listened to the wet gurgle of his intestines spilling out; they were hanging down to his knees now and the blood was pumping out like a fan in front of him, in a spray, as if he were a red lawn sprinkler.

When he finally sighed, a little frothy blood even came out of his nose, the left nostril, daubing his upper lip. And then he slowly sank down to his knees and doubled over forward, his curly head hanging down. He was crying.

She closed the razor and got off the bed, and she took the razor into the shower with her. She scrubbed for a long time under the hot water, then patted herself dry with one of the fluffy monogrammed towels.

She walked through the bedroom, not looking at him, and went into the living room. She looked around until she found the right closet. Both bags were there, still carrying the E W R tags. Her denim pants and bush jacket were there; her shoes, her purse. Her underwear had been thrown down on top of the shoes. She opened the smaller bag and got out some fresh underwear, lacy beige underpants, and stepped into them and tugged them up. Then she picked out a brassiere and shook it out, holding it by the shoulder straps. She looked at it for a minute, and then put it back into the bag. Then she put on the rest of her clothes and looked around the apartment.

She found the glass that she had been drinking from at the party and washed it off carefully, using lots of soap. And then she went back into the bedroom, edging past the bed.

The towels and everything would be fine; she used one to wipe off the edge of the mirror and the handle on the toilet. She used another towel to open the medicine chest and take out the flat leather case. She put the razor back into the Tuesday slot and snapped the case closed and put it into her jacket pocket.

On the way out, she paused and looked at him one more time.

He was still on his knees by the side of the bed, hunched over, his curly head down between his shoulders, his lap all full of his stomach. It covered both hands. The intestines were mostly white-gray, lined with kind of purple veins.

He was still crying. Not breathing. Just crying.

five

"SOMETIMES," the sergeant said, "you forget just how much stuff is all crammed inside your body until you see one all laid open like that. You know, you would think you can't get that many guts in there and just hold them all in place with a layer of skin across the front. The blood, well, you kind of expect that because blood goes everyplace."

The doctor merely nodded, wiping his hands; he was not as impressed with the mess. The area just around the bed smelled faintly like warm raw liver.

"So how long's he been dead?" the sergeant said.

"Mmmm." The doctor shrugged. "I don't know. Maybe at least twelve, thirteen hours. Hard to tell. He's already locked into position like that. No use trying to straighten him out here. You could hoist him up from the floor and bury him that way, on his knees like that; just tuck all that junk up into his arms. It would save space."

The sergeant lit another cigarette and looked around the room. He looked up at the ceiling, and seeing a cherub, swung his head around to make sure that there was one in every corner. He was still new on homicide. He was thirty years old now, nine years on the force, and he could make lieutenant in, say, another six. Well, if he could hold everything together that long. He was blackhaired, underweight and generally considered at Zone Three to be very smart. "Come on in the other room a minute," he said.

"What are you doing here anyway?" The doctor picked up a

bottle of Dry Sack from the bar. He held it up to the light and looked at it, shook it, then pulled out the cork and sniffed at it. And then he took a clean glass and poured some into it. "You heavies never come around these things at first. Me, I got to."

"Listen, that stuff is evidence."

"So all right. So fine. Your guys have already gone over all this stuff in here anyway. It'll still be evidence; just one little shot less evidence than before, that's all." He sipped at it. "Care to join me? Very civilized, as we say. We say that a lot."

"No. I don't know, maybe I should have been a doctor. You guys always drink in the middle of the day. Anyway, why am I here? How do I know? All I know is Harvey Olsen called me over at the office and said it looked interesting. Now I'm not so sure. It looks messy, that's about all. So tell me what you think."

"You want me to solve this thing for you? Easy. First, you know that his dingus was cut clean off, right? It's there on the floor beside him, somewhere underneath all his insides. That was the first cut. Sliced away almost his whole left nut along with it. Very clean. *Snick*. Like that. It was the second cut did all the work, though."

"What with?"

"You got another cigarette?" The doctor put the sherry down on the bar and patted at all his pockets. "Thanks. Uh, you got—"

"Here, for Chrissakes." He lit the cigarette for him and clicked the lighter closed. "You sure there's nothing else around here that you need? You want to go through the dead guy's stuff here? Maybe he's got a shirt or something that'll fit you."

"Okay, then, where was I? Oh, uh huh. Right now I would say maybe a thin-bladed switchblade. Good, limber steel. You know, very sharp; very, very sharp. I'll know more later after we take him apart more. Possibly a kitchen knife, but I doubt it could cut that smoothly. And wielded by a strong, steady hand, as they always say."

"Who says?"

"Well, look, both cuts are so clean. Especially the main one. The guy who did the cutting didn't sort of start *here* and then pause in the middle or anything like that. The slice goes too smoothly. It must have been like a nice, big golf swing, the way Nicklaus would cut you with a sharpened five iron. It caught the victim right here, between the old iliac crest and the inguinal ligament. Zip, like that. Some skin, you can always tell if it's been sawed at. Not here."

"It looked all kind of curled up around the edges to me."

"That's now, and that's natural enough. I'm talking about *then*, when it was done."

The sergeant nodded. "Uh huh. So go on."

"Okay. I'll give you your slasher. This place is up to *here* in drugs, right? Lots of really exotic stuff, too, not just street things, and all of it expensive. And look at the furniture; the bar here, those couches. This stuff is Sloane's at the very least, probably even better. Now, the place also is full of nightgowns, for Chrissakes, trick, sexy stuff like that. So, one, your guy in there is a pimp. Sure, high-class. Expensive and all that. But a pimp."

"Oh, I don't know. I'd say that chances are a lot better that the dead guy wore all the nightgowns himself. You see his hair?"

"Oh, no. Uh uh. You go for the pimp thing yourself, I can tell. So, back to one. He's killed by a rival pimp. What could be easier? Case closed. God, I should have been a cop."

"Maybe a rival pimp. Or how about a dissatisfied customer?"

"Do they ever?"

"How about a hooker, then? Say, one of his girls?"

The doctor poured a little more sherry into the glass and put the bottle back behind the bar. "No way. You know that better than I do. First, all of them are on drugs themselves. Half the time they're out of their tree and all the time they're not strong enough to do something like this. They spend too much time all strung out and they sit around a lot waiting for the main guy to come home and beat the shit out of them. Besides, if it was a hooker, she'd have shot him. They all do. Stabbed, maybe. Possibly. But never cut like this."

"But what about the cut-off schwanz?"

"I don't know about that. I guess maybe it seemed like a hell of an idea at the time."

"Uh uh. Wrong again. Any guy would tear up forty miles of turf to keep from getting his dong cut off. There's no fighting in here, right?"

"Sure doesn't look like it, right."

"Well, then." The sergeant walked back over to the door and looked into the bedroom. "No, it's got to be a . . . well, it's not a rival pimp. Or if it was, our man here didn't know it was a rival. Or whatever; that's too complicated anyway. There doesn't seem to be a hell of a lot of sociology involved here, really. It's two queers. One queer wore the trick nightgowns and the other one did all the cutting. It figures that the first thing he would cut off is the other guy's cock. That part adds up. But—"

"I know. But the part you can't get is why our guy just stands there and lets the other guy do it. It's not your standard sort of sacrifice."

"Mmmm hmmm."

"Well, then, you see? That's the part that makes you the ace cop and me just a daytime sherry drinker. You're the one who gets to go out there and shag this guy down. He'll have the switchblade hidden in with his lingerie, probably. It'll turn out to be from Abercrombie's. Fish-filleting model."

"Thin blade, though. Whippy."

"Uh huh, right. And save it for me when you get it. I can always use a knife like that down at the shop."

They left it at that.

He stayed in the apartment after the crew had gone, walking from room to room, smoking and carrying an ashtray in one hand.

He stood at the foot of the bed for a long time, looking down at the twisted sheets.

"Should be satin," he said.

He opened the closet again and looked in at the clothes. He lifted out one of the gowns, red velveteen, and smelled it, then put it back with the others. He went into the bathroom and opened the medicine chest and looked in at everything. Then he closed it and went back into the bedroom and lit another cigarette.

He reached down and picked up the shirt from the floor and smelled it, first down the front, then under each arm, and threw it back down.

Finally, he looked at his watch.

Okay, then. Fine. This was exactly the payoff for letting the mistaken goddamn impression get around that he was smart. A comer on the force. A thinker, which is even worse.

He looked around again, looked back at the bathroom door. All right. So something was decidedly ass-end-to. Which was certainly natural enough; things are forever fucked up in some way. There was something that he couldn't see—even if he was probably looking straight into it. Or it was something that should be there and wasn't. Well, either way, he didn't have the faintest goddamn idea what it was.

He leaned over and put the ashtray down on the foot of the bed.

Hell with it. The thing was, after so many of these, after standing in so many damn apartments and looking down at so many bloodstained Rya rugs, it was hard to get pumped up anymore. What the hell difference would it make? None. He straightened up.

Maybe he would go in and have a glass of that sherry after all.

six

"THERE'LL ALWAYS BE a little scar right up here, see? That's where he hit me the hardest time," Nancy said. "I swear, he kept right on hitting at me until finally I had to let go of the purse, pulling back and forth with it like that. But I guess I can comb my hair down over it. See? Sort of like this. Well, never mind. I'll get it done. It's either I've got to wear bangs the rest of my life or go around always telling everybody about it."

Gloria nodded.

"But the rest of it is just a matter of waiting for the swelling to go back down. You should have seen this eye right at first. I mean, if you think it looks bad now."

"It's greenish-purple," Gloria said.

"Mmmm hmmm. But at least I can see out of it some now. And other than that, I just plain hurt all over and I got to get all new credit cards."

They were in Nancy's apartment now, on the fifth floor, closed behind the upper sentry lock and the lower Yale lock and safety chain and the chrome-plated wedge stick that braced up under the doorknob. The music was on, the Judy Collins, and they were drinking Gallo Hearty Burgundy with ice cubes in it. They were both sitting on the floor with their elbows up on the coffee table.

"Anyway," Nancy said. "Uh, anyway, you still don't want to talk about it?"

"Come *on*."

"All right, all right." She shrugged. "So don't. Hand me the wine instead. I just thought that maybe it'd make you feel better. That's all I mean. Like you don't have to give me every little *de*tail; I mean, like what wonderful things you two *did* to each other and things like that. Or did the earth move or anything. I meant, you know, just in general."

"In general," Gloria said, "in general, I've already told you. I mean—"

"Sure. Uh huh. You got into town, right? You found out that I was in the hospital. And then you just disappeared for four days. And then you show up here, ummm, what? Sadder but wiser, I guess that's what. That's pretty general, all right."

"Come on. I told you more than that."

"All right. I know. You met a guy and you had an unhappy experience. Some of us, it takes years in this town to work up to an unhappy experience. Or at least all summer. You could have maybe called me just once while you were so busy getting unhappy and I wouldn't have worried. Good thing I didn't call your folks or something."

"I did call once. The hospital, I mean. But they had already let you out, I guess."

"You didn't either," Nancy said. "You want some more ice?"

"Mmmm. Listen, are there any munchies in there, too?"

"You're a munchie." But she started pulling things out of the refrigerator. And then she raised her head back up and looked over the door. "I suppose he was married. They always lie about that. Sometimes I think you ought to make all men empty out their pockets before you even *talk* to them. You know, look inside their wallets for pictures of kids on Shetland ponies or something."

"I don't really know if he was married," Gloria said. "But I don't think so. Anyway, do we have to talk about it anymore? Come *on*. Soon as I get it all settled in my head, maybe I'll tell you all about it. Lord, it was flat dumb to get into a mess like that, and I'm still too damn mad. But we've really got to leave it at that. I met a man and I disappeared for a little while and I'm sorry. But that's all I want to tell about it. Someday, maybe . . ."

Nancy put the tray down on the table and began spreading cream cheese on the crackers and then handed one over. "All right, all right. Never mind. Here, eat this. And let's just forget it, all right? I was just trying to make you feel better, that's all. Wait a minute, I can only spread these damn things so fast. Anyway, I'll never bring it up again. That's it. All I got to do now is to sew a scarlet A over the left boob on all your blouses."

"Mmmm, I really like these wineglasses with the big bowls like this. Anyway, the way you sew, I'll already be an old lady and it won't matter."

"And here I was going to show *you* the town and all when you got here. You've probably been everywhere already."

"I didn't go out much," Gloria said.

"And introduce you to a couple of men. Lord knows, they're not up to much; pretty awful, in fact, but they're about the only ones I can get my hands on right now. Maybe you can introduce *me* to—"

Gloria scowled at her. "Look, is it okay if I turn on the news? It's time now."

"Sure, go ahead. See if they caught my mugger yet, that dirty bastard. Listen, I eat any more of this cream cheese and I'm really going to get sick, I promise."

"Let's eat out someplace. After the news, all right?"

"Okay, then. One more."

Gloria propped both elbows on the coffee table and held the wineglass by the stem with her fingertips, rubbing the bowl part across her forehead to feel the cool.

All right, then. Breathe calmly. The thing was, there probably wouldn't be anything more on the news about it now, not after all this time—and especially not in New York. These folks here kill each other constantly. But still, she had to watch for it every evening, holding her toes curled down inside her shoes, trying not to look directly at the television set, but sort of obliquely, peeking around the bowl of the wineglass. It is a thing you can do if you know about something in advance, see; if you figure it's going to happen, you just flat *anticipate* it. Then you're prepared. You're on guard and you can steer it away in advance. Otherwise, it's liable to surprise you, and then you're caught. But not if you know; not if you're ready.

She had been watching for it practically ever since she had gotten to the apartment. She had slept a whole day and a night first. And then, when she finally did see it on the TV—with Nancy talking on as loudly as she did—she had been able to mask the flush of anger. She had sat there, gone all prickly, taking a sip of her drink, lighting a cigarette, shaking the match a lot and then missing the ashtray with it, nodding back at Nancy, anything.

There had only been a flash of him on the tiny screen. It looked like a picture taken from his college yearbook or something. His hair was different, all straight and parted on one side, no beige curls or caramelly look; goddamn him, he had probably gotten it done in some beauty shop or something. But it was him, all right, that dirty son of a bitch; the smile, the eyes, everything.

With Nancy talking, Gloria hadn't heard it all. The reporter had said something about "socialite" and "posh Park Avenue bachelor apartment" and something else about "victim of a savage attack" or something like that. And that's when Nancy had said, "There. See what I mean? Good God, you even get mugged in your *own* apartment around here. Besides, why don't they catch *my* mugger, answer me that? Hell, I *know* where he is. He's in Bloomie's, putting suits and things on my charge card, that's where he is."

Then the *Times* had had it, a sort of medium-sized story on an inside page. But Gloria had read through it so quickly, shaking, that right now about the only word she could remember from the whole story was "Dartmouth." The *Daily News* had put his picture on page three, and this time he had all the tawny curls and he was wearing a tuxedo, but you couldn't really see his face too well. He was standing with a scrawny girl; her two neck cords stood out in front and she was wearing gold lamé bib overalls and way too many bracelets. They were both holding drinks in their hands and there was a painting on the wall behind them, and the caption said that it was last year at the Sculls', whatever that was. The story was really one of two that had started out on the front page under one big headline. It said:

PARK AVE.
SLASHER

And under that, in smaller type, there were two more headlines. They said:

PLAYBOY SLAIN   KNIFE HEIRESS
(Page 3)   and   IN GEM HEIST

Nancy had brought the paper home from work and had left it

on the couch. Gloria had been making coffee when she first saw it, and then, reading the headline from across the room, she suddenly really had to go to the bathroom. She had sat there on the cold toilet seat and wet and wet a lot, curling down her bare toes on the tile floor, looking at her hands and listening to the pounding splash she was making. And finally she had gotten up and turned on the cold-water tap and dabbed some water on her forehead and then had gone back out and picked up the paper.

The picture on the front page was of some fat old lady wearing a tiara. She had been robbed at knife point in her Park Avenue apartment; a whole big bagful of jewels. And when she had put up a fuss, the man had cut her across the shoulder.

The other story said that the bachelor playboy had been slashed to death after a party at his place and that he had had a lot of parties. His body had been found right beside his bed, kneeling down as if he had been saying his prayers when the killer struck.

Two slashings on one street, a few blocks apart. And that was it.

And now, nothing more on the news. It was all over now. Well. There were some more murders on the news, sure, but they were just plain murders, that's all.

"You ready?" Nancy said. "They're only going to do the weather next anyway after the commercial. Come on. Look, does this seem all right combed down like this? It's about the best that I can do right now. What do you think?"

She shrugged. "Looks fine. Okay, I'm set. Let's go."

"I swear," Nancy said, "it sure isn't easy being a sex goddess, right?"

Gloria looked at her again. Nancy had always had the best of it. She had never been all stringy and had to worry about things like elbows and kneecaps. Nancy had started out cute right from the beginning and she had pretty much gotten everything to stop growing all at the same time, right at the cheerleader part. Little turned-up nose and turned-up little tits; in fact, Nancy had probably peaked back in those days when she was twirling around in a pleated skirt and showing off her ass on the basketball gym floor. But she was getting too heavy now, hunky across the thighs, and from the back you could see the doughy rise of each buttock, each one clearly traced by panty line. And now, with her hair all patted down in front like that, she looked sort of like Mia Farrow with a walnut in each cheek or something.

"What is it?" Nancy said. "You sure this looks all right? Or should I comb it back again?"

God, what the hell difference would it make? One thing, the city sure hadn't changed Nancy a lick. She was *here*, but she was still hanging on to her high-school cutes, the cornpone and honeysuckle stuff and all.

"You don't like them," Nancy said. "The bangs."

"No, no. I was thinking about something else. It's okay like that. Makes you look like Mia Farrow."

"We're about the same size, you know. Well, I'm maybe a little bit taller, I don't know."

"I know. You said it before."

"But you think so?"

"Oh, for Christ's sake," Gloria said. "Let's go get some dinner, all right?"

They ate at the House of Chan again, on the corner of Seventh and 52nd, sitting in the little back dining room off the bar, holding the fantail shrimp by the tails and dipping them delicately into the trick curry sauce. Gloria figured that, getting this late a start, she would maybe never get enough fantail shrimp. If folks had something like a lifetime quota of fantail shrimp that they had to make up before they died, well, she was way back. Oh, they had shrimp in Oklahoma, sure, but not big, fat buggers like these, all split up the center and then fanned out and all deep-fried like these. "Are you going to eat that last one?" she said.

Nancy shrugged. "Do I get a choice?"

"No. I really want it."

"Jeez, I'll sure be glad when you get on to your next food phase. Here, take it. Can we maybe eat someplace else next time?"

Gloria shook her head no, chewing. And she lined up the little hollow tail alongside the others on the plate, pushing it into the half-moon pattern she had built.

"How's it going at work now?" Nancy said.

"Mmmm, so-so. I mean, you know. The job is easy. But none of the men are very good-looking. I don't know, they're all sort of, uh, rumpledly."

"Naturally. And chauvinistic, too. But that's the way it is at *Time*, see? *Newsweek*, too, I suppose. Hell, any magazine. In fact, a girl in my study group is from *Newsweek*. Same old thing, she says. I think the idea is, if you're a writer, you don't get to be smart and pretty at the same time. It's the . . . whatever they call it. The law of compensation or something like that."

Gloria nodded, picking up each tailpiece again and looking down into it to make sure it was really empty. She was working on *Time*'s library clip desk now, which was the best that Nancy had been able to do for her, but she was learning as fast as she could and she had put in to become a researcher. The researchers had the really good jobs—checking facts, looking up things; all organized, putting a little red line under every word in every story. Best of all, they each had little offices of their own with those sliding frosted-glass doors and name tags and all. And they could afford the Sisley jeans with all that nice stitching.

Still, right now she got to read and file everything in its right spot, and then deliver research all around the floor, the red subject folders full of clippings and stuff. And the men writers and editors would all look at her a lot whenever she came into their offices. Well, wait. Not those sort of narrow-eyed looks like she had gotten back there in the terminal, like she was for sale or something. But different. These were pure looks, all nice and open. First, they would look at her top and then, most of the time, the look would move slowly down to the brass button at the waistband of her jeans and then follow the seam right on down to where it went under and out of sight, lingering at that part. But always, they looked straight into her chest, as if each one of her breasts was a kind of big, round sun giving off warmth from inside her blouse.

A couple of the writers always went heavy-eyed, like maybe they wanted to lean right forward and nuzzle her, maybe to put one side of their cheek against one of them and rub it softly back and forth. And one of them, Barry Harkner, if he would only ever get on with it, for God's sake—she would let him. Sometimes in the bathtub at night she thought about it, about standing there beside Barry's desk with his office door closed behind her. She would have to take charge or they'd never get it done; he needed that. She would let him bury his nose and his whole face right here, here between them, and then she would hold the back of his head so lightly with both of her hands, fingers all mixed into his hair, and she would turn his head slowly so that he could kiss first this one, then the other one. Here, on the inside part. And here.

Barry was really big and sort of shambling and fuzzy, like he was always just a teeny bit out of focus. His shirt was never tucked in right. But he talked in a soft, low voice that made her vibrate right here, right at the wishbone, where her ribs came up and joined together. He was married.

"Glory, we're all married," he had said. "The standard approach for men around here, I believe, is to say that you are married but separated. Or married and not getting on with your wife and, therefore, harboring a growing animal need. Or that you need the comfort of an intelligent woman for a change; your wife has no *idea* of the things you go through. Well, as it happens, I am none of the above. I am married and married; that's it. And I dearly wish that you would stop coming in here looking like that."

Well, all right. That's what he said now. But maybe if she . . .

"You all right?" Nancy said. "I told you six dollars and forty cents and you looked right through me. And you're breathing through your mouth again. Look, just put down the money and let's go on home."

She gently pushed the shrimp tails back into the pattern. "Okay," she said. "Let's go."

They had just turned the corner by the deli and were walking down toward their building when they saw the car.

"There he is again," Nancy said. "See?"

It was a Lincoln-something, all shiny, with what looked like a pebbled-leather rooftop, and it had mirrors and bright things all over it. The man got out and looked up and down the street for a minute, then walked around to the other side and opened the door. He was wearing a red silky suit and red platform shoes; the tips of his shirt collar were fanned out over the lapels of the suit and the shirt was unbuttoned to his waist. He half bent over and got the girl by the arm and helped her out.

She was young; no, really young, and her hair was frizzed out on both sides and stringing way down past her shoulders. She was wearing dirty jeans, all frayed around the bell-bottoms where they dragged against the sidewalk. And sandals. With striped socks inside the sandals, for God's sake. She was carrying a faded red canvas knapsack, holding it by the straps and letting it drag. She was smiling up at him.

"See?" Nancy said. "About the third or fourth time he's been around here. Pimp. You'll never see that in Oklahoma, right? Different girl every time he shows up. Yuck. He must really *like* dirty little old white girls like that. You see her hair? Lord, she can't be any more than, say, seventeen or so. And he's—"

"Fifteen, maybe."

"Uh? Fifteen what?"

"Years old. The girl. She just looks like that because she needs scrubbing up. You know."

"Well, anyway. It's still awful. Maybe we ought to call up the—"

"No, you don't," Gloria said. "Look, this is your town, not mine. And you said this happens all the time. Come on."

But in the elevator, while Nancy talked, Gloria took deep, heavy breaths, quietly, taking the air in through her mouth and puffing it out through her nose. And in the apartment she stood at the window, looking at the Lincoln down on the street while Nancy got undressed, still talking.

"You think I ought to go and get the bangs done tomorrow? You know, the Mia Farrow? I'll have to call first thing in the morning if I do."

She didn't turn around. "Go ahead. Make you feel better anyway."

"And I might even have him streak it a little bit, too, huh? You know. Frost it?"

"Mmmm."

"Okay, I'll do it. Everything locked?"

"Mmmm."

"Chain and all?"

Easy, now. "Yes, uh huh."

"Okay. See you in the morning, all right? Your turn on the coffee."

"Night."

Gloria put the heels of her hands together, fingers up, fingers down, and pushed hard, looking down at the Lincoln. Then she curled the fingers on both hands and locked them and pulled apart hard with each arm, breathing deeply. She could feel the strain on her pectorals.

Finally, he came out of the hotel alone. He looked around the street again, and he reached into an inside coat pocket and took out a handkerchief and wiped the palms of his hands on it. And then he walked around and got into the car and drove away.

She brushed her teeth and went to bed.

But she got up again at 1:45 A.M. and went to the bathroom and then walked into the living room and stood at the window. The Lincoln was back down there, parked a couple of spots from where it had been the first time. She waited.

This time another man came out of the hotel and walked a few steps and then stood there. He was in some kind of a uniform; a soldier, maybe, she couldn't tell from this far up. Then he seemed to spot the Lincoln and he walked over to it and put both hands on the doorsill and leaned over and looked in. He reached into one pocket and took something out and looked at it and then handed it inside the car where she couldn't see. Then he walked away and turned out of sight around the corner.

In a minute, the Lincoln's lights came on and it pulled out. It waited at the intersection, the turn signal blinking faintly.

She went back to bed. She tried closing her eyes tight, until little pinpoints of light shot all through the inside of her eyelids. Then she tried half opening her eyes and tracing the lines of cracks in the plaster ceiling.

But she kept right on thinking about the little girl with the dumb frizzed-out hair.

seven

"No IMPLICATION WAS INTENDED, ma'am," the sergeant said. He put the pictures back on his desk, face down. "It's just police procedure, that's all. We have to—"

"Sergeant," she said, "my son did not have an enemy in this world. None. Nor did he consort with gangsters, those . . . those awful men there with the numbers around their necks. I certainly do not recognize any of them and I would certainly hope not to. And another thing, you smoke entirely too much, Sergeant . . . mmmm . . ."

"DeMario," he said. "Antonio DeMario. And I'm aware of that, ma'am."

"And further, of course I didn't approve of his rather, well, his rather wild life-style. What decent mother would? But the fact remains that he was my son and he was murdered. You are aware of *that*, I trust?"

He nodded, looking at her. And then he shook out another cigarette and lit it and breathed in deep. "Yes."

"Well, then. I don't seem to see a great scurrying around here in search of the murderer. You, all of you, seem to reflect a certain sense of apathy. If any sense at all. Exactly what is being done? Aside from sitting here looking at these ugly pictures."

"I assure you, things are being done. This is a big city; these things often take—"

"And what is more, although it seems ironic for me to bring it up now, I have never been fully informed of the circumstances of my son's death. The newspaper accounts were lurid, I'm told, but they were kept from me. That is none of your concern, of course; it represents my family's regard for my age and physical condition. However, I have not been told exactly how he died, beyond the sketchiest possible information. Certainly not by the police. And not by our own hometown funeral director, who refused to discuss it. All right. Now that I am here, I demand to know. It is my right, of course. I must . . . Sergeant, I am talking to you."

He stamped out the cigarette, looking across at her, then shook his head no.

"Yes, ma'am," he said. "I can hear you. However, I would certainly not want to go against the wishes of your family. You must try to understand. Sometimes these things are for the best. Hearing the details would only—"

"Don't talk down to me, young man."

"—only . . ." He stopped and blinked. "All right. I'll stop. The fact is, he's *dead*. What difference does it make how he got that way?"

They looked at each other for a long moment. Then she got up, leaning one hand on the desk for support. "I see. Well, then, I assume I may go now?"

"Of course. I'll have a man take you—"

"You needn't bother."

But she turned at the door and looked back at him, her mouth drawn tight. "De*Mario*, is it?"

"Yes, ma'am."

"Italian, I take it?"

"I'm afraid so, yes. Italian."

"Hmmm. A heavily bearded race, the Italians. One thinks of blue jowls. And by what means do you shave, Sergeant De-Mario?"

He blinked. "By what means do—"

"You *do* shave, of course. Well, then, what do you use to shave *with*, Sergeant? May I presume to ask that rather personal question?"

He stood up. And then he walked over to her. She had one hand on the door. "Just what is it you're getting at?" he said. "Uh, ma'am."

"What I am *getting* at, young man, is that I do not have all of my late son's personal effects. I have the list right here with me in this pocketbook. And conspicuously missing from the number of things returned to me are his antique razors. They are—" She looked at him closely, frowning. "You seem suddenly flushed, Sergeant. Not a sudden flush of guilt, I would hope."

"No," he said. Then he paused. "No, just flushed. Please go on."

"Well. The razors are quite valuable. Not in terms of money, I suppose, but in an heirloom sense. They—"

"*They?*"

"They. Please pay attention to me. You look suddenly distracted. There is a *set*. In a monogrammed leather case. One razor for each day of the week, of course. They belonged to my father, God rest his soul. He had them made in London; he left them to his only grandson. And now they are missing. Which means that someone has to have them. And I want them back."

"And you think—"

She nodded. "I do, indeed. I have been told that certain police officers are not above appropriating certain private property for their own use. You do read the newspapers, of course. Official corruption is rampant in this city; policemen *flout* the law. They steal. And don't look at me like that. Perhaps you might better look deeply into your own conscience, Sergeant. Seven razors. Genuine pearl on the handles, of course. Blades of the finest steel, I would imagine."

"Lady," he said, "I would *bet* on that part."

"Hmmm?"

"Never mind," he said. He reached around and opened the door for her. "I'll look into this matter right away. In fact, I *promise* you I'll look into it. And it was ever so nice of you to come by."

He walked back to the desk and plopped down. And then he jabbed at a cigarette butt in the ashtray, twisting it down into loose shreds of tobacco.

"I'll be a son of a bitch," he said.

He pushed all the papers around on his desk until he found the property list.

Contents of apartment. All right. Where? Contents of the bathroom. Contents of the medicine chest in the bathroom. Uh huh. He had read the list too damn many times now anyway. But there it was, where it had been all along. One aerosol can of shaving lather. One electric razor. *Electric.*

He picked up the phone and dialed and waited. Then: "Olsen," he said, "DeMario."

"How you?" Olsen said.

"Never mind. Listen, the Park Avenue thing, right? You with me? The curly-haired pimp."

"The curly . . . oh, yeah. You mean old blood-and-guts."

"Right. You went through all the stuff up there and made up the list I have here, right?"

"Uh huh. Yup."

"You got your notebook?"

"Just a sec. Okay, wait. No, I got it."

"Okay, then. The bathroom. Got that? The electric razor."

"Uh huh. Yup."

"What kind was it?"

"I don't know. Ummm, let's see. Oh. A Schick."

"That's it?"

"That's it. A Lady Schick."

"Lady?"

"That's what it says here. Yeah, I remember seeing it up there. A *Lady* Schick is what women use to shave their legs and stuff. You know. They can also shave their twidget with it if they want to do a baldy."

"Their what?"

"Shave their *thing*. You know, their crotch."

"Are you kidding me, for Christ's sake?"

"No. Some women, they like to—"

"That's not what I mean. What I mean is how in God's name am I supposed to know that it's a LADY goddamn electric razor when I see it on the list here? How am I supposed to know that?"

"Well, I didn't put it down by design or *type* or anything like that. I mean, what the hell difference does it make, anyway? He had ladies up there in his apartment. He was a fucking *pimp*, Sergeant, remember? I suppose they used the razor for shaving their legs and stuff so as not to scratch the customers. You know."

"Your ass, I know. It turns out that that was the one thing I had to know and I didn't know it. Now, get the hell over here. We got work to do."

He hung up the phone and looked at the list again.

That was it. Shit, he should have figured it out. Well, maybe he should have. You see electric razor on the list, you have to figure like anybody would that the guy is shaving with it. But, no. It was for some girl or something, and there was the shaving lather, which meant that the guy was shaving with . . .

"Dammit," he said. "If it isn't one damn thing, it's something else. A straight-edge razor. Nobody has killed anybody with a straight-edge razor in this town since the year of the blue snow."

eight

"Now, YOU SEE?" he said. "Aren't you having a good time? Have I pounced on you yet, tearing at your garments?"

She shook her head no, looking into the bowl of empty black mussel shells and breathing deeply. Then she tore off a piece of the bread and dropped it into the juice to let it soak.

"Listen, Bear," she said, "will you tell your wife about this?"

"I really wish you wouldn't call me Bear. My mind always reels between the connotation and the spelling. I keep getting the image of myself naked."

"All right. Barry."

"Thank you. And as for your question. You mean, will I go home and stand at the ice bucket and offhandedly say, 'By the way, dear, I had a lovely lunch today with a statuesque girl named Gloria Cooper.' No, I won't. No need. I'm terrible at this. What will happen is that I'll simply creep home wearing a look of absolute guilt and she'll know."

"Then why did you ask me out to lunch?"

He nodded at the table. "To try the mussels, as I said. Well, that's my excuse to me. For one thing, I certainly won't have to tell anybody *what* I had for lunch today; they'll know the minute I get off the train. See, the thing about the mussels here at this restaurant is that the effect comes on slowly. Then, later, they make you glow in the dark. Wonderful. The aura clings to you for days, defying all underarm sprays and colognes. People turn away from you at staff meetings, coughing a lot."

Gloria smiled at him. "They're really good, just like you said. But why, really, I mean?"

"Well, I'm not exactly sure. Every time I see you standing in my office, everything goes blank. I seem to suffer some sort of brain fade, looking at you. Other than that . . ."

"I like looking at you, too."

"There it goes again," he said.

They had walked over to the Tout Va Bien from the Time-Life Building, with Barry hulking along sort of splayfooted, heading west on 51st Street, one side of his shirt collar curling out over his sport coat and his shaggy hair blowing all around in the wind. She had held his hand each time they crossed the street, then let it go.

At first she had said no. He had looked up to see her standing there with the research files. Then he had leaned back in his chair and explained about the mussels at the restaurant he knew, watching the look on her face while he talked.

"We don't have mussels in Oklahoma," she said. "I've never had them. But then, we don't go out to lunch with married men in Oklahoma, either."

And then she had walked all around the hallway, her head down, looking at the carpet. She had gone into the ladies' room and looked at herself in the mirror, out again and back around the hallway to his office. He was sitting with his chin in his hands when she looked in.

"All right, I'll go," she said.

And now she carefully lifted the piece of bread out of the juice and shook it a few times and popped it into her mouth. "Boy, you won't have to tear my clothing," she said. "A couple more of these bread things and it'll start to fall off in shreds."

He leaned back, nodding. "You know, you're a complicated girl, Gloria-Ann."

"But glamorous, right? You know, European, like."

"A bit glamorous, yes. But not very much. No, mysterious is more the word. Smoldering. There is an undercurrent of—mmmm—intrigue and—"

"That's me."

"—and, I guess, the promise of dark passions. Like Rita Hayworth in *Gilda*. If I might make that rather feeble comparison."

"Who? *Gilda* must have been before my time."

"Don't remind me," he said.

"What else about me?"

"You have an astonishing figure," he said. "I don't know how you do it."

"More."

They looked at each other again. "I can't seem to think of anything else to say," he said.

"Well, I just want you to keep right on talking," Gloria said. "I don't really care what it is you say; I just like to listen to the—uh—the hum of it. It makes me feel good."

"Where?"

"Right here."

He glanced down at where she was pointing. Then he raised his eyebrows a bit. "Perhaps it's the mussels," he said.

"All right. Anyway, it was a good lunch."

"It was all those things you say. And more."

"Can we do it again?"

"Yes."

"Will it make you feel all guilty?"

"Yes."

"Every time?"

"I'm afraid so, yes."

"Then we won't do it again, Bear."

He sighed. "Yes, we will," he said. "Yes, I'm afraid we will."

nine ━━━━━━━━━━━━━━━━━━━━━━━━━━━━━

THE SERGEANT WALKED down the hallway, past the janitor's closet and the men's room. He turned right and entered the office. The meeting was already under way. "Sorry I'm late," he said. He put his raincoat down on top of his typewriter, reached across his desk and picked up his mug and looked down into it. It was dark brown and sticky on the bottom. "Is there any more coffee left?"

The lieutenant nodded. "Christ sake, DeMario, you could just fill that thing up with hot water and get the same stuff, way you take care of it. Leaving it out every night like that. Besides, I think the lady dusts it with that feather thing. Anyway, hurry it up. We're just getting to you. Where you been?"

"Overslept again." He poured the coffee and went over and sat down behind his desk. He patted at the raincoat until he found the cigarettes, reached into the pocket and got one. "I do that a lot since the divorce. There's not a hell of a lot else you can do in one room."

"But you get laid a lot," Olsen said.

"That's just the rumor around here. What I really do is think about getting laid a lot."

"I've been up in your room, remember?" Olsen said. "Smells like a girls' gymnasium up there."

"Look," the lieutenant said, "if it's all the same, can we just get on with this? Come on. Now, where was I?" He looked down at the open file in his lap. "Okay. Cohen, Bradford, that's all for you guys. Only thing else I can think of is to go back over there and question some more people. Get somebody to help you out with the Spanish. Ruiz? You busy today? Okay, go help Cohen and Bradford. Now, then. DeMario. Olsen."

The sergeant held the mug in both hands, his elbows on the desk. He nodded and yawned.

"Am I keeping you up, DeMario?"

"I'm up, I'm up."

"All right. I've been reading your DD-Fives here. Most of this stuff seems fine; just keep going. And, let's see here. These two. The torso. The one from in front of the restaurant. Well, I don't know what else to tell you either, except that I guess we just wait for some of the other parts to show up someplace. You talked to all the garbage-men, it says."

DeMario nodded.

"And the restaurant guy," Olsen said. "All he knows is that the bag showed up there that morning with all the others."

"And you looked in all the other bags."

"Uh huh. We both did. Nothing in there but old hog jowls and stuff. You know."

"Don't make me any sicker than I am now. I just ate over at that place last week." The lieutenant turned the report over and picked up the next one. "Okay. The pimp, right?" He looked over at the sergeant. "You say here you think it was a razor now, a straight edge. Okay, fair enough, way the guy was cut up. Anything else?"

"No. That's about it."

The lieutenant closed the folder and stood up. "All right. Something'll turn up. Just don't spend too much time on this so you can't keep up with your reports, okay? You're behind especially, DeMario. I don't know, maybe you better stay in and clean up your desk today; Olsen can go out. Okay?"

"Fine by me," Olsen said.

The lieutenant looked at DeMario and then pointed to his own office. "In there," he said.

They walked in and the lieutenant closed the door. He walked around and sat behind his desk. "You all right?"

DeMario shrugged. "I guess. No. Sure I'm all right."

"Like hell. Losing weight. Your goddamn pants hang on you; you don't eat right. And here I come in and find out that you were in here half the night last night. What? Working on things.

What the hell, DeMario. Back off a little. Look, people get divorced. It happens."

"I know. It's not the divorce. That's all over now. Well, assuming I can ever pay off her attorney; that part. But I'm fine. Stop worrying about me."

"Want me to reassign some stuff?"

"No. Not yet."

"Some time off?"

"No."

"Olsen okay to work with?"

"Olsen's fine. His reports—he writes very funny reports, in fact."

"Swell. One goddamn lieutenant, four sergeants and forty detectives in this zone and I got a guy who writes funny reports. That's what I really got to have. But okay. Listen, sure I worry. What the hell. You're probably the smartest guy I got over here and you're going around looking like something the cat dragged in."

DeMario sat down on a chair and stretched out his legs. "All right, so I'll get my pants taken up in back. But listen. Can I ask you something?"

"Sure. Ask, already."

"Well . . ." He looked down at his hands. "Well, did you ever used to get bored?"

"How do you mean?"

"I'm not sure. No, yes I am. I think it's the city; well, a city this size. I wanted this division. Fine. I finally got over here. I passed the exam; I made sergeant. Thanks to you. But . . . well, I used to get fired up about things. But it's getting harder now. I find myself standing in some bedroom, or some alley someplace, looking down at somebody who has just recently had the top half of his head blown off, and I find myself thinking that it's all *cyclical*. It keeps going around. Ahh, it's spring, right? Time for somebody to beat somebody to death with a bicycle chain again. You know. Or all the junkies or dealers lying at the bottom of stairwells with their pockets turned inside out and chipped plaster in the wall behind where they were standing when the bullets came through. Shell casings lying around. All that. Look, I got a desk full of all that stuff out there in the room. Same stuff: you use a knife, you use a razor, you use a gun. You just change the names, that's all."

The lieutenant nodded. "I know, I know. But what the hell, DeMario. You work in a small town, you end up counting Buick hubcaps in the evidence room and thinking, shit, I've done all this before. Look, it's the same everywhere; it's just a matter of degree, that's all. Sure, I used to get bored. I get bored now. Christ, *you* got it all over *me*. You're single now and you can get around. Get laid; get some strange stuff. Me, I got to go home to Seventy-ninth every night and my goddamn kid is in her room smoking pot and the dog has chewed another leg off one of the dining-room chairs. I'll show you *bored*. What you got to do is just hunker down and go through with it and then, pretty soon, you get numb. And as soon as you get numb enough, they make you a lieutenant. Okay?"

"Okay," DeMario said. "I just wanted to know, that's all."

"You're no different than anybody else. But you ought to be smart enough not to let any of these cases get to you."

"Okay, okay. Cold and unfeeling, that's me."

"That guy's mother gave you a hard time. The pimp guy."

"Christ, I'll say. I would have punched her right in the fucking nose. Except that I think maybe she could lick me."

"Well, I told you, don't get personally involved in any of this crap. Just stand off and do your job. Run 'em in and run 'em out."

"Got it."

"You sure about the time off?"

"Yes."

"Fine. Failing that, get the hell out of here and go get yourself some breakfast. Don't go where they put the torso in the plastic bag. But somewhere. Eat, will you?"

DeMario turned at the door. "Listen, thanks."

"One more thing," the lieutenant said.

"Hmmm?"

"Is it true you're getting laid a lot? Like Olsen said, I mean?"

"No. It isn't true."

"Well, you might try that, then. I would. Goddamn, how I would, if . . ."

DeMario smiled at him. "All right. I'll work on it."

ten

He bent in close, so close that when he whispered, it ruffled the hair covering her ear. And she could smell the—uh—the what? His sort of warm crème-de-menthey breath from the stingers. "What's wrong?" he said.

"I don't *know*," Gloria said. "Honest, Bear. No, wait just a second. Don't do that any more just yet, all right?"

He took his hand away.

Lord, Lord, come *on*. Let's go. She had finally decided to go ahead and do it—and now this. And she had even told him that she had decided to do it, too, so that there wouldn't be all the dumb goddamn fumbling around with snaps and zippers and things. And now she was having trouble breathing and, if she knew her damn stomach, she was probably going to be sick pretty soon.

"What is it?" he said.

"Goddamn it, I don't *know*. Really."

"Is it me?"

"No, Bear, me. It's me."

Christ, oh, dear. And he was so beautiful, too. All big and soft all over and apologetic. And gentle. And now she figured that she had really known maybe a couple of dates ago; no special time, really. It wasn't like being run over by a car. She had just flat looked at him one moment, somewhere, and had realized that she was going to get him down and let him *do* it to her. And if he didn't do it to her, she sure as hell was going to do it to him. And right then, when she got around to admitting it to herself, she knew inside her head just exactly what he would look like with all his clothes off, and what he would smell like and all; everything. He probably had a smallish penis. He looked like it from the outside. And then, for the last day or so, she had even pictured in her mind just how she would set it up: Nancy would still be gone on the assignment, and she would bring Barry up here. And then she would turn out all the lights except the bathroom light. And then she would take everything off and leave the bathroom door open just a little crack, and she would stand right over there and the backlighting would be perfect. He would see her just all in furry outlines; the light would make a soft halo up and down her thighs, like fire. And he would sit there for a minute, just looking, and then he would come across the room and get her.

But, no. They had locked the door and gone directly to the couch before she could do any of those things; even before she could go in and add some more spray cologne. Then, after they had kissed and had kept on kissing and feeling each other all over, she had told him that they were going to do it.

He had thought about it, first looking at the backs of his hands and shaking his head, and then looking at her closely. "You're sure?" he had said. "You're shaking."

"I know I'm shaking. Never mind that. I really want us to. Right now. I've . . . well, I've done it before."

"But not much."

"No. Not—uh—not much, no."

And then he had leaned back, shaking his head some more and looking at the ceiling. "Glory, love," he had said, "will you tell me what I'm doing here? I missed my train hours ago, and I didn't call home. It's just as though there isn't any home; it's out there somewhere on Long Island and I can't even remember it. I can close my eyes and I can't even remember what my wife looks like. Well, no. Small breasts. And rather thin-lipped. Stern-looking. But—"

"Barry, don't," she had said.

"No. Let me start over again. I'm here. Slinking about guiltily in some apartment on the near East Side of Manhattan. Here with all the swinging singles. I don't know. Maybe there's still time. Look, I want to do it. I have *wanted* to do it ever since I first saw you. I'd like to do it every hour on the hour. God, I'd like to walk *around* in it, carrying a lantern and looking at all the furry scenery down in there. I'm probably in love with you, whatever that means. Certainly I'm on fire for you. But we can wait. Really, now. We can—"

"Bear, please," she had said. "Just hug me some more."

And he had, until they were both breathing through their mouths harder and harder. He had talked gently into the soft spot on the front of her throat, right here, so that she had to listen hard to hear him, and the hum of his voice just seemed to ooze into her. "I don't know," he had said. "I feel like some sort of—ummm—a test case or something. No, I don't mean testing *me;* not an audition. But I feel as though you are testing you. Does that make sense?"

"Bear," she had said. "Bear, just stop *talking* and put your hand right here. No, here. Down inside."

And now. Now. Shit, oh, *dear.* She sat up and readjusted the waistband of the panties, snapping it hard. And they were the Pucci's, too, the blue-on-green print, eight dollars. She had wanted to look just right for when she decided. "You'll have to go, Bear," she said.

"I thought as much. Are you going to be all right?"

"Mmmm. Not really."

"Can I help?"

"Absolutely not."

He buttoned his shirt up the front, then unzipped his pants and tucked it in all around. "Two hours or so in a cold shower and I'll be just as good as new," he said.

"I'm sorry."

"I know, I know. Look, it's all right, really. Just try to remember what I look like without a shirt on. Fix it in your mind. Next time we'll try to get to the pants. And then socks and shorts. It isn't much, I know, but it's a body you'll be seeing more. A body without a home at the moment. I can always sleep on the couch in my office."

"No, it's a fine old body, don't say that," Gloria said. "Besides, I probably love you a little bit too, you know. I mean, men are bad. No, men *can* be bad. They do—"

"But not me. At least you can't say that I tried to drag you right off to bed."

She nodded. Damn, her stomach hurt. "I wanted to do it. Really, Bear. I really wanted us to, but I just can't. I don't know what's the matter, but—"

"See you at the office," he said.

She redid all the locks, snapping and clicking them. And then she went into the bathroom and leaned over the toilet bowl, looking down into the water, until she decided that she wouldn't be sick after all. She would be *something*, goddamn it, but she wouldn't be sick. Maybe what she would be was goddamn good and mad.

She walked back into the living room and picked up her skirt and her panty hose and shoes and then walked over to the window and looked down.

The Lincoln was parked down there again.

That son of a bitch. She breathed in deeply. And that meant that little old dirty miss goddamn dumbbell was still in that hotel there. And it meant that the pimp was there, somewhere. Maybe inside, beating her up. Maybe sitting in his car there.

She leaned her forehead against the glass and kept looking down, waiting.

eleven

THIS WAS THE WAY everybody said to do it in New York: have some coffee and the cheese Danish right there in the delicatessen at eleven o'clock. It always spoiled your appetite for lunch, and if you had a date that night, you could save the money from two meals that way and maybe buy the blouse at Saks if they still had it. She stirred the cream into the coffee with the little wooden stick and put it down on the marble-top table. She picked up the Danish and turned it around a few times, looking closely at it, and then she took a big bite where it curved out wide before it got to the cheese part.

"You're supposed to cut those and eat them with a fork," Nancy said. "More ladylike."

Gloria nodded, chewing, and then took a big swig of the coffee and mushed everything around inside her mouth.

They both looked out the window again. They were watching the girl.

She had been there on the corner when they had walked down to the deli from the apartment building. She was wearing black double-knit hotpants now, with a tiny white quarter moon of buttock hanging out on each side from the back, and black vinyl boots that came up to her kneecaps, and a loose-weave black knit top. Her breasts bobbled around loosely inside it, with the blunt little nipples clearly defined, perking out. She was wearing big dark glasses with pink frames. Her hair was still frizzy.

Most of the men were brushing right past her, looking sort of sideways at her breasts. The few who stopped just said a couple of words and then walked on, shaking their heads no. Between men, the girl would glance over at the cars that had stopped for the light at the intersection. A few of the drivers looked at her, half smiling. But when the light changed, they all drove on.

"Bad corner," Nancy said.

"Not only that, it's cold out there," Gloria said. "Look. Her little old ass is getting all blue. Lord, why can't somebody—"

"Like who?"

"—somebody do . . . Huh? *I* don't know. Someone. Good God. Listen, you and all that big talk about the National Organization for Women. Well, *some*body ought to be able to do something. Jesus. Hell, in Greer . . . listen, if this was *Greer*, she'd be off the street in about two *minutes*. Old Lester Mumfort would flat come and grab her the second she stepped out*side* in that getup. And the *man*. Huh. Christ's sake, just one time, one *time*, that pimp would show up in town with those trick red platform shoes and Lester would flat shoot him. And—"

"Well, don't bark at me," Nancy said. "It's me, remember? You've been like this for a couple of days now; ever since I came back from the assignment you've been like this. Come *on*. All this snapping and snarling all around. If it's the cramps, I sure wish you'd get it over with. Anyway, look, cuz, I know what old Lester would do, and shooting the man would be just fine. And nobody in Greer would say a thing. They'd stand around and pull at their suspenders and nod, I guess. But not in New York, you can't."

"Well, look at her," Gloria said.

"I see her. And she's freezing."

"Well, hell, that's what I'm telling you. It's not her fault. I mean, she's about fifteen and she's *dumb*, that little dummy, and she's been *had*. Lord, everybody must be dumb in this town. Folks go around doing awful things to each other and nobody does anything about it. You know that? Listen, you want to know where the *man* is? The fancy man? He's probably sitting somewhere in his fancy trick car with the heater turned on and listening to the tape deck or something. That's where he is. How about that? And *that's* where you got to do something about it, where you got to start. Not some little old kid here with her buns hanging out."

Nancy nodded. "You want some more coffee?"

"Lord, I guess."

"Another one of those things?"

"No. Barry is taking me out to dinner tonight."

"You going to bark at him, too? Or is he the cause of your cramps?"

"I don't HAVE cramps, Nancy. That's next week, not now."

"All right, all right." She put the coffee mugs on the table and sat down again. "Anyway, someday I suppose I'm going to get wood poisoning from these damn stirrers; they're like little tongue depressors. Yuck."

Gloria pointed again. "Look there. See? That cop just walked right on by. Just flat walked past her. And nobody's going to do anything. You keep saying you're working on it. Sure, but—"

"We are, we *are*," Nancy said. "Now, don't get all hot again. I mean, me and the national organization and all. Well, all right. It may not be much, but you've got to start *some*where. I'm not going to start marching around in those stupid tinted aviator glasses or anything; you know, batik blouses. And I'm still going to shave under my arms. Look, I'm pretty and I'm feminine and I'm going to stay pretty. Even you admitted that I look a little bit like Mia Farrow. But the thing about the national organization is, well, it's still growing. It's getting some things done, too. It all just takes—"

"Uh huh. Well, what about her out there? And what about pimps?"

"Shhhhh. Listen, Jesus, Glory. I mean, there's *equality* to worry about. Equal pay for equal work and all. And we're getting it, too. You do what you can at first. It's slow going, sure. But if enough women . . . well, you know. What do you have against them, anyway?"

"Because they're not going *fast* enough," Gloria said. "And they march in those bullshit gay liberation parades and all. Marching along there with the queers, laughing at everybody standing on the sidewalk watching them. You know. Or they picket the Playboy Club or whatever. Lord, I'd be embarrassed."

"I know, I know. But we'll get to—"

The girl pushed open the door and walked in. She went directly to the counter where all the trays of meats and salads were lined up behind the glass, standing on her tiptoes to look across at the counterman. She ordered hot chocolate. She took it to the little table next to Gloria and Nancy and sat down and poured a lot of sugar into it. Then she got out a cigarette and lit it. Her hands were shaking.

Gloria took a deep breath and half turned in her chair.

"No, *don't*," Nancy said. "No. Come on."

But Gloria leaned forward and looked at the girl, until she looked back, blinking.

"You shouldn't let a man *do* you this way," Gloria said. "I know what it's like and it's *bad*. You're too young and too little and all."

The girl paused, the mug halfway to her mouth. Then she lifted it the rest of the way and took a sip, looking back at Gloria. She put the mug down and picked up her little purse and stood up. She reached around and tugged her hotpants away from one buttock, shaking her leg a little. And just at their table she paused, looking first at Nancy and then at Gloria. "Git oudda heah," she said. And she went back out through the door.

"Good *God!*" Nancy said. "What did you have to go and do THAT for? Jesus, I could have fallen right through the *floor* when you really turned around there and talked to her. Did that solve anything? That make you feel any better?"

Gloria nodded. "Some," she said.

"Well, we better go. Finish your coffee there. I swear, cuz, I don't know what I'm going to do with you. Christ, you're getting more militant than me, even. Well, anyway. We'll go on back and I'll vacuum if you'll do the tables, all right? What time is Barry coming?"

Gloria tied the cashmere coat in front, getting the belt just right so that the two ends hung down carelessly. "Ummm, I don't know. Seven-thirty or so, he said. Anyway, soon as we get through with the cleaning, I'm going to go on over to Saks and get that blouse I saw."

"Okay. But you need another shirt like—"

The man came in and then stopped short, standing in front of the door. This time he was wearing a robin's-egg-blue silk suit and dark-blue patent-leather platform shoes. When he smiled at them, the teeth were all white and big and perfect.

"Hey, baby," he said.

"Excuse us," Nancy said. "Come on, Glory, we got to go."

But he held up one hand, the palm toward them. The palm of his hand was lighter colored than the rest of him. "Like, wait up here. I jus' got a little question for you. Which one of you ladies was jus' hasslin' my little woman in here? I mean, like, how'm I gonna know, since all you honkies look jus' alike to me, you know."

Gloria looked at him. She slowly pulled on her kidskin gloves. Then she opened her fingers wide and punched at the gloves carefully in between the fingers to make them fit tight. Their eyes were exactly level. He was slender, standing with his pelvis swung out; his genitals were outlined clearly where the shiny blue pants fit tight up between his legs. He was still smiling.

"It was me," Gloria said.

He reached over and flipped one of the ends of the belt on her coat, then caught it in the air and tugged gently at it. "Nothin' serious," he said. "Now, doan look so *mean* at me, lady. I jus' wanted to say to please not, like, you know; don't hassle my woman, 'cause it make her nervous. You unnerstan' and—"

"Let go of the belt," Gloria said.

"—and all, okay?"

"Maybe you didn't hear me, pimp," she said. "The belt."

He looked into her eyes for a long second, and then he dropped the belt and patted it where it was tied. And he stepped to one side as they went through the door. "You ladies be sure an' have a nice day now," he said.

They walked down toward the apartment.

"I think maybe I'm going to faint," Nancy said. "Or scream or at least wet my pants or something. In fact, oh, God, I *did* wet my pants just a little bit there. Weren't you scared or anything?"

Gloria kept looking straight ahead, breathing deeply. "No."

They did the whole apartment after Nancy changed her underwear, vacuuming and dusting all the tables. Gloria did the dinner dishes from the night before and stacked the wineglasses upside down on the rack to drain. Then she went into her bedroom and closed the door. She leaned both elbows on the dresser and looked at herself in the mirror for a long time. And finally, she nodded back at her image.

And then she opened the closet door and got down the little bag from the shelf on top. She put it on the bed and unzipped it all around. She reached inside and got out the flat leather case with the initials. She unsnapped it and looked at all the pearl handles nestled there in the black velvet. Then she lifted out her razor and slipped it into her front right-hand pocket. She put everything back.

When she came out of the bedroom, Nancy was sitting on the couch, feet tucked up under, doing her fingernails.

"I'm going now," Gloria said.

Nancy nodded, waving one hand to get it dry. "Have a good time," she said.

twelve

SHE WATCHED HIM pull the little girl up the steps. He was holding tight to her arm and shaking at it. She waited until the door swung closed behind them and then she walked out from under the awning and across the street and up the steps. The glass on the front door was dirty and the gilt letters that spelled out H O T E L were chipped and scratched. She stopped in the small foyer; there was no front desk, just a cardboard sign with MANAGER penciled on it and an arrow pointing down the hall. The place smelled like cold cabbage. She waited, listening, breathing evenly. Then she turned and started up the stairs.

At the first corner, where the stairs turned to continue up to the next floor, the slapping sound got louder. She stopped and stood still, looking up into the darkness.

She could hear the girl yell loudly once. Then there was a pause, and then the rest of it was just the girl crying in bursts and saying, "Please, don't do it" while she was being hit. And then it stopped.

She waited, listening. And she slipped her right hand into her pocket and lifted out the razor.

When the door opened in the hallway above, she sank down to her knees on the landing where the carpet was all frayed, holding her right hand in her lap and patting at the floor with her other hand. The door slammed closed and she could hear the footsteps. He came clomping down around the corner. She didn't look up. She could see the toes of his shiny blue shoes.

"Hey," he said.

Gloria looked up at him, squinting. "Wait just a second before you step around here," she said. "I just lost my contact lens."

"Hey," he said. "Come on. You in my *way*. I'm in a hurry."

"No, please. You'll step on it."

She looked down again and started patting at the carpet with her left hand.

"Dark in here," he said. "Can't find no little old bitty piece of glass down in the dark there. Come on."

"Well, could you help me, maybe? It'll just take a second and then you can go. Look, you pat with your hands like this. Lightly, see? You can always tell when you feel it."

"On my *knees*? Are you funnin' me? Man, I'll get my pants all dirty doin' that stuff." But he hunkered down and made a few pats. "Contack lens. Huh."

Now she turned slightly, moving her knees an inch or so at a time, still patting at the floor, until he was directly opposite her left shoulder. She eased her right hand out of her lap and moved it down out of sight against her thigh. And she rolled her hand over to open the blade.

"Come on, lady," he said. "Ain't no jive-ass contack lens down here. I got to go."

"What's this?" she said.

"Where? I don't feel nothin'."

"No, no. Over here. Put the tips of your fingers right here."

"Aww, come on. I gotta . . ." But he leaned far out, putting his weight on both hands, feeling the carpet. And when he looked up at her, the spot was right.

She swung her arm around hard and the blade caught him just under his left ear. She lifted up quickly, rising into a crouch and slicing across hard. She brought her left hand up fast and grabbed a handful of his hair and twisted his head around sharply to the left and finished the stroke near his right collarbone, bending her wrist back to do it. Then she stiffened her shoulders and pulled him forward, slamming his face down and skidding it across the carpet until the top of his head hit the wall of the landing. She stood up.

The blood came boiling out and she stepped down one step so that it wouldn't hit her shoes.

He braced both hands against the floor as if he were doing a push-up and raised up to his hands and knees. He hung his head down and shook it several times. He began to cough and the blood started to come out of his mouth and nose. Then, slowly, he rolled over until he was half leaning against the wall, looking at her. The stain was fanning out across his chest, spreading down darkly under his arms. He began moving his mouth to say something, but it was just making blood bubbles.

Then he slumped farther, settling slowly into the corner. His hands were open loosely now, palms up, with the fingertips slightly curled. His legs went apart in the tight blue pants.

She stepped back up on the landing and stood over him. "Goddamn you," she said. "You got this coming, you hear me?"

And she leaned down and slashed him twice across the abdomen, once this way, then coming back, swinging the blade hard and bearing down right into the inside of his crotch. Then she wiped the blade on his pants leg, using both hands, carefully getting off all the blood. She held up the razor and checked the pearl handle for spots.

She turned and walked back down the stairs and stood in the foyer, listening. She put the razor back into her pocket. And she went out the front door and turned down toward Saks.

thirteen

THEY STOOD ON THE SIDEWALK in front of the steps and watched. The two officers locked the wheels of the stretcher into place and then closed the doors on the black panel truck. One of them came back over.

"Anything else?" he said.

The doctor shook his head. "No, I guess not. Go ahead and leave him in the rubber bag when you get him there. You know. I'm going to go play handball first anyway. I'll look at him tonight."

The man nodded and went back to the truck. The doctor put down the zippered white Adidas gym bag and straightened and turned up the collar on his raincoat.

"So much for your theory on the queers," he said.

The sergeant looked back over his shoulder at the hotel door. "Yeah, I suppose. I don't know. It wasn't much more than a hunch anyway. So much for you and your goddamn switchblades. Or what was it you said?"

The doctor shrugged. "Filleting knife. You know, like at Abercrombie's. But you want to talk about doing some plain-and-fancy cutting like that up on the stairs there, it's a good old straight-edge every time. Christ, those things scare me to death. Worse than scalpels any time. Hell, my hands shake just changing the blade on my *Trac Two*. A straight-edge and I'd cut off half my mustache and probably my lower lip. But anyway, yes. It looks right now like a razor, all right. Like one of those seven you said. I mean, I can't go down there and look at the cuts and say 'Well, that's *Saturday*,' or anything like that. But straight-edge, sure. You figure it's the same guy did this?"

"Now how in the hell would I know? *Here*, you got a cut throat to start things out. But then, you've also got a disemboweling, and disemboweling is not exactly the In thing around here this year. Cutting right through the guy's schwanz and all, just like over there on Park Avenue. Tell me that's coincidence."

"Hell, I'm not going to tell you anything. I'm going to go play handball."

"See you around."

The doctor picked up the gym bag. "Sure. Go careful when you shave, DeMario."

The sergeant turned to Olsen. "I thought they shut this place down, the vice guys."

"They did. I mean, they do. This isn't really all that bad a neighborhood. You know. The residents get hot about this and they get up a block association and all. Couple pross arrests and we come in and lock the doors. But they got this attorney, you know, the little guy who does their stuff, and he goes to court and they do an end-around on us and they open it up again. Happens every time."

He lit another cigarette. "How many hooks work out of here?"

Olsen looked at his notebook. "I don't know. A bunch, it looks like."

"How many pimps?"

"Four, five. Maybe less, I don't know."

The sergeant nodded. "Well . . ."

"What are we looking for, Tony?"

"Hmmm? What are we looking for? Well, what we are looking for, pal, is a guy carrying around seven straight-edge razors. And that's if we're *lucky*. If we're *un*lucky, what we're looking for is seven guys carrying one razor each."

fourteen

"You know," he said, "you really a *bad*-looking fox. You know that? I mean, some kind of *bad*. Oh, yeah. I'm not jivin' you. Get you out of them dungarees and into a nice little old *dress* or something. Little tiny skirt and all. You could be in the *business*, you unnerstan' what I mean? You'd be *fine*."

"How can you tell in this light?" Gloria said.

"Look, *I* can see jus' fine. You the one who's doin' all the squinting. Now, you sure you dropped the lens right down here?"

"Uh huh. Keep patting. No, not so hard. Contact lenses are really delicate."

"Gotcha. Like this here? Anyways, what you doin' here, big fox? I mean, this here is a *mean* hotel. Mean. That's why I got these suitcases here. Like, I'm splitting."

"I came up to see a friend. Why?"

"Why? There was a dude *murdered* here the other day. No, I'm not jivin' you. Like, it was one landing down; you know, down there where you just come up from. Blood splashed on all the walls, man, blood running down the *stairs*. And that poor cat laying there all snicked up. All that. Not me. Uh *uh*. I'm not working out of no hotel where cats get cut up on the *stairs*. Not me."

"Wait. I think I found it," she said.

"Where at?"

"Right here, I think. You got a match?"

"Match? A *match?* Listen, I got me a *Dun*hill, fox. Huh. They give matches *away*. Look at here."

She waited until he had his arm extended, clicking on the gold lighter. She rolled her right hand over and opened the razor. And then she feinted to her left, her knees braced far apart, and swung her arm around fast.

The blade hit him just under the ear and went into the carotid artery. She put her shoulder into the move and started pulling the razor across.

He snapped up his left hand quickly, a catlike, blurring strike, and grabbed her wrist. The razor bounced out of her hand, glanced off his shoulder and fell to the carpet behind him.

"Sheeee-*it*," he said. "Ohhhhh, God." He let go of her wrist and put his hand to his throat, the fingers spread wide. The blood began pulsing out between them, down over the back of his hand. Then he closed all the fingers, trying to palm the blood. "Gah-*damn*," he said.

She arched backward when he swung at her with the other hand, hitting the side of her head against the landing wall. His fist came by right at her collarbone.

"God," he said. "Awwww, *God*. You cut . . ."

They got to their feet together. He was a little shorter than she was this way, crouched over, holding his throat with one hand. The blood was spilling out at the butt of his hand and was running up his coat sleeve. He clenched his other fist again and started to swing, looking up at her. There was a wide diamond ring on the little finger of the fist.

He wasn't as fast this time; she ducked under his fist easily, leaning forward, and reached around behind his leg and picked up the razor from the stair. She took her time, moving carefully. She got it just right in her hand again and got the blade all balanced. He began pounding her on the back with his fist; she could feel the diamond ring digging in across her shoulders. Splashes of blood began dripping off the front of the bandanna she had tied over her hair. She reached over under him and braced her left hand against the wall. And then she straightened up fast, slashing up with the blade. It caught him just at the inside of his thigh and came on up through his crotch as she turned, pressing upward.

She stepped back and looked at him.

"Mama," he said. "Mama. God, I can't . . ."

He swung around, toppling the suitcases out of the way, and started back up the stairs, dragging his shoulder heavily against the wall. He was leaving a smear.

She waited, watching him lurch up out of sight around the corner, and listening down the stairs. Then she stepped around the puddle and walked up after him, watching where she put her feet.

He made it halfway down the hall, then fell to his knees, both hands clutching at his genitals. She walked around in front of him and stood there, her legs spread apart, until he looked up at her. His eyes were fogging over and he was breathing froth through his mouth, spitting it out on his chin. She put the flat of her right foot against his chest and pushed him over onto his back.

"Pimp son of a bitch," she said.

She kicked his hands out of the way so that he lay spread-eagled. And she leaned over, swinging her arm around like a scythe, and slashed him the other way. When she straightened and stepped back, he slowly curled himself into a fetal position, pulling his legs up. His feet were twitching.

She pulled off the bloody bandanna and stuffed it into her pocket. Then she checked her pants legs for blood, lifting first one leg and then the other. She looked at her sleeves closely and then took off the jacket and folded it over inside out to carry over her arm. Then she stooped and cleaned the blade on his pants cuff and flipped it closed. She stood, turned and started back downstairs. At the landing near the two suitcases, she paused, listening. She looked down.

Like he had said, there was blood running down the stairs again.

fifteen

"YES, I KNOW," the sergeant said. He had the telephone cradled against the side of his face, hunching up his shoulder to hold it in place while he opened a pack of cigarettes. "Yes, lieutenant. No, I . . ." He lit a cigarette, listening, and then glanced over at Olsen, sitting in the chair beside the desk. "No. In fact, we don't really. No leads at all. Nobody saw anybody. But then, nobody ever sees anybody in those hotels. You know." He snapped his fingers to get Olsen's attention and then he put the thumb and forefinger of his right hand together to form a circle. And he slid his left index finger in and out of the circle a few times in a screwing motion. Olsen nodded.

"Yes, I read it," he said. "Yes, I know. Mmmm . . . I know. But we can't help that. They must have got it off the Unusual Occurrence Report and then talked to some people on their own. No, they didn't get it from any of us. I know. But, listen, to be perfectly frank, that sort of story treatment has to be a natural for them. No. No, wait. I'm not trying to be funny, lieutenant. No, *I* didn't say Jack the Ripper. The goddamn *Daily News* said Jack the Ripper." He looked at Olsen again and shrugged. Olsen shrugged back. "Yes. Yes, I'm all too aware that it can make us look bad. All too aware, I assure you. Yes, yes. Of course. Around the clock, yes. And I'll keep in close touch, sure. And I hope you're feeling better, lieutenant. You know what they say: drink plenty of liquids and take some aspirin and try to get some rest. No, no. I'm not trying to be funny again. No. Good night, sir."

He nodded and hung up the telephone.

"Work around whose clock?" Olsen said. "You told me I could have off. One more night on and my old dragon throws the switch on me. Besides, you said."

"I know I said. Well, go ahead. Christ, there ought to be a rule around here against married cops."

"You think I'm gonna argue against that? You make the rule, DeMario, and I'll use it. Look, I'd rather work all night. Besides, you were married once, too, you know."

"Olsen, everybody was married once. That's not the point. The point is, I did the honorable thing. It came down to being married or making sergeant and she had to go, that's all. Besides, she never really liked me in plain clothes. She liked the belt with all the shells in it."

"I know. Christ, I got to wear the whole rig to bed, piece and all, or my old lady can't get it off. Look, I'm going, all right?"

"Go ahead."

Olsen nodded at the telephone. "Does he know it's still a razor?"

"Sure, he knows. Well, if he read my last DD-Five, he knows. The *Times* doesn't know. The *Daily News* doesn't know. They're still running off about surgeon's tools and operating-room stuff to go with their Jack the Ripper thing. They'll all find out sooner or later. Not that it really matters."

"So what's next?"

"I'll tell you in the morning. Go on home. Do your bed time. Get it over with."

He waited until the door closed and then he pushed the chair back and swung his feet up on top of the desk. He reached over and got the gray file folder and put it in his lap.

All right, then. He read through the newspaper clippings first, skimming.

Modern-day Jack the Ripper stalks New York. Slashing, hacking. Disemboweling his victims with clean, surgical precision. Horseshit. *Wreaking some sort of mad vengeance on pimps.* Fair enough. Better pimps than cops. *Sprawled in the hallway of the dingy hotel when found, blood pulsing from the cleanly severed arteries in his throat.* More horseshit. Who writes this horseshit? *Scalpel. A surgeon's knife. Only someone with an intimate knowledge of anatomy, said the expert, who asked not to be quoted by name. Struck down by surprise. The flash of a scalpel in the dimly lighted stairwell. Intestines.* Oh, for Christ's sake. He was getting pretty fucking fed up with intestines. *Jugulars cut. Blood sinking into the worn carpet. Police fan out in search of killer.* True. Well, more or less. *A number of good leads, says Sgt. Antonio DeMario, in charge of the investigation.* Definitely false. *Psychopath.* Well, that seems reasonable enough. *Mad doctor.* They're all mad, for Christ's sake.

He moved the clippings over to the other side of the folder and picked up the DD-Five from the morgue officer and read it again. He put it on top of the clippings and picked up the wound charts and looked at the drawings. The locations of all the cuts on the bodies had been drawn in with a felt-tipped pen. He fanned them out and looked at all three, then put them face down in the file. He picked up one of Olsen's typed reports, a condensation taken from the doctor's protocol that had been recorded on tape during one of the autopsies.

> The razor incision starts at the region of the anterior superior spine of the iliac crest and goes medially and inferiorly in the direction of the inguinal ligament, penetrating the full thickness of the abdominal wall, striking the symphysis pubis, then transecting the base of the penis and the anterior portion of the scrotal sac, so that the shaft of the penis is totally severed, and the anterior portion of the scrotum with the vascular and ductal structures being severed. The wound continues onto the left thigh, entering the medial aspect of the leg, severing the sartorius muscle and exposing the vastus medialis and the structure of Hunter's canal, <u>viz.</u>, the femoral artery and vein and the saphenous nerve.

All right, then. So much for an intimate knowledge of anatomy. Mad surgeon, my ass. A goddamn belly is a belly every goddamn time and this was just a plain old swinging slash. He leaned forward and fumbled around on the top of the desk until he felt his cigarette pack, then shook one out and lit it. He picked up Olsen's condensation of another of the medical reports and read it, squinting through the smoke.

> There is a wound in the neck that starts
> one and one-half inches below the left ear-
> lobe and passes medially and inferiorly
> across the neck, measuring six and one-half
> inches in length, causing a gaping of the
> anatomical structures, to wit: sternocleido-
> mastoid muscle is transected in its anterior
> half, the external jugular vein is severed,
> as is the whole carotid sheath, with the in-
> ternal jugular vein, vagus nerve and the
> carotid artery. The wound exposes the sev-
> ered thyroid gland and enters the thyroid
> cartilage in its lower one-third. On the
> right side of the neck, the wound continues,
> severing multiple small muscles, the thyroid
> gland and the anterior half of the carotid
> sheath, severing the jugular vein and one-
> half of the carotid artery. Muscle bundles
> have retracted, leaving a gaping opening. It
> is estimated that exsanguination and death
> resulted in one and one-half to three
> minutes.

One and one-half to three minutes. Shit, that's not even enough time to say goodbye.

He swung his feet down and put the open file on top of the desk. He took off his sport coat and hung it over the back of the chair, then walked over to make sure the outer door was locked. On the way back to his desk he took a key out of his pants pocket. He unlocked the top right-hand drawer and took out a book. He sat down again, swung the chair around and put his feet back up. Then he got a notebook and pencil and adjusted the desk lamp. He put the book and the notebook in his lap and started to read, underlining certain passages and taking notes in the notebook.

It took him three hours.

He locked the book in the drawer again and then read back through the notes. His head hurt and he was out of cigarettes now, so he picked through the ashtray until he found a suitable butt and lit that.

He went back to the Park Avenue report again, thumbing down to Olsen's interviews. Olsen did good interviews, always typing in all the comments and everything.

INTERVIEW WITH DOORMAN

Doorman: Several people came in or out that day in addition to the regular tenants. They included:

Big Guy. Old. White hair. Wore it long, like a senator.

Two Society Ladies. Little white dog. Dog peed where he had just polished that brass over there. Could kill that dog.

Medium-sized Guy. Pansy. Levi pants made up of a bunch of denim patches. Visits here often. Good tipper; a buck when you get him a cab.

Big Girl. Two suitcases, one big, one small. Didn't want a cab. Would be pretty if not so mean-looking. Can't remember the hair; blond, maybe. Walked down Park toward 58th.

Black Guy. Long nightgown thing and one of those trick hats with a tassel. Looked to be a U.N. guy. Tipped a quarter for a cab. Got his dress caught in the door. Serves him right.

Big Girl. Very short skirt. Big thighs. No chest to speak of. Orange fingernails. Walked down Park toward 58th.

He put the report to one side and went back to the notes that he had taken from the book, rereading them slowly.

And then he picked up the pencil and turned back to Olsen's doorman's list.

And he put checks in the margin in both places where it said *Big Girl*.

sixteen

AFTER THE MAN HAD CALLED from downstairs, she went into the bathroom and ran the basin full of cold water. Then she held the tips of her fingers down in it, looking at herself in the medicine-chest mirror. She was breathing hard. She raised her hands, shook them once, and pressed the tips of her fingers against her temples.

Nancy came and leaned against the door. "Are you all right?"

"Me? Of course," Gloria said. "Why?"

"Why are you doing that?"

"What?"

"That. Doing like that with your fingers."

"Oh. My head's hot."

"Who was that on the phone?"

Gloria looked at herself in the mirror again, pressing down with her fingertips. "It was the man downstairs. He said two policemen are in the building here. They're questioning folks, you know, to see if they can help on those killings across the street."

"Oh, that. Big deal." Nancy swung away and walked back into the front room.

Now then. Ease up here and get your dumb blood all settled down. She took a few more quick breaths, going over all of it in her mind, rechecking all the details. It's just like with the news on television that first time: get all the possibilities fixed in your head so that nothing will surprise you. Just anticipate every-thing. And when it comes . . . well, if it comes at all, then you can just flat turn it aside. And get your goddamn face set right.

What it was was just two plain old policemen asking questions, right? Well, what could they know? Okay, then. Let them ask.

The buzzer rang.

"I'll get it," Gloria said.

She wiped her hands on the sides of her pants and went to the door.

"Check first," Nancy said. "Don't just haul off and open it."

She moved her eye closer to the peephole and looked again, then pressed down on the little button to talk. "I don't care about the badge," she said. "Anybody can carry around a badge. I could go down to the dime store and get a better-looking police badge than that one."

"Don't let him in," Nancy said.

Gloria turned back, her hand covering the peephole. "It's two of them. It's got to be the two cops that the doorman said. Wait a minute." She bent down a little and peeked again, then swung back, nodding. "They don't look especially like policemen. I mean, they're not wearing police suits. You know."

"That's what I mean. Find out first."

She pushed down on the talk button again. "Let me see the I.D. cards," she said. "No, that's too close up. Back up just a little bit so the light hits it. Okay, then. Now the other one. Mmmm hmmm. Okay, just a second."

She undid the chain, then twisted the upper lock back and unclicked the Yale. She opened the door.

"Welcome," she said.

The tall one nodded, smiling at her. He was wearing a blue blazer with silver buttons and a tie with little red whales on it.

"Hello," he said.

"Hello."

"You certainly do have a lot of locks."

"Mmmm."

"No, it's all right, really. And you did exactly the right thing, making sure of our identity. I wish everybody was that careful. Okay. My name is DeMario. Detective Sergeant Antonio DeMario, Third Homicide Zone. This is Detective Harvey Olsen, who follows me around a lot. Now, may we come in for a minute?"

He really had white teeth. Not white translucent, but dog

white, like a refrigerator door. When he smiled he looked wolfish and very smart.

She shrugged, stepping back. "I'm Gloria-Ann Cooper. No, no, just come on in. And this is my roommate, Nancy Marie Cavanaugh. Well, actually, it's Nancy's apartment and I'm her roommate, I guess."

"Glory?"

"No. It's the accent, I guess. A lot of people get it wrong like that. I'm working on it."

"Well, don't work too hard," the smaller one said. "I could listen to that kind of soft talk all day long. I mean, in comparison to what we hear all the time. You know."

"What part of the South?" the sergeant said. "Memphis? No. Atlanta."

"Lord, no. *South.* No, it's Oklahoma."

He grinned at her again. "Shows you what kind of a great detective I am. Oklahoma. Sorry. I was even going to say someplace farther south. Louisiana, maybe."

"It's really a soft accent," the one named Olsen said. "Nice."

"Well, I—"

"Oh, for God's *sake,*" Nancy said. "All right, all right. So much for the magnolias and all that. Come on in and sit down. You-all look like a raid or something, just all standing around like that. The doorman said you were coming. What can we do for you?"

Both men sat on the couch, both bending forward at the same angle. The sergeant turned the ceramic ashtray around with his fingerprints. "May I smoke?" he said.

Nancy shrugged. "No, go ahead. Can we get you something to drink? Some coffee? There's some red wine and maybe one shot or so of Wild Turkey, I think."

"Some coffee would be very nice. Thank you."

"I'll get it," Gloria said.

She looked back in at him from the kitchen. His hair curled over his shirt collar in back and the rest of it was all wavy and sort of walked-around-in. He looked strong for being so awful skinny, hunched up over the coffee table like that. It was the way he held his shoulders forward.

"What do you-all want in it?" she said.

"Go ahead and use the mugs," Nancy said. "I can't stand seeing men with big hands holding those cups and saucers."

"Just black," the sergeant said. "Please."

"Everything in mine," Olsen said.

Gloria waited for it to heat, watching the sergeant's back some more. He looked like he cut his own hair, probably with kitchen scissors. Or maybe he just sort of rumpled it dry that way and put on his clothes. He didn't look particularly married or anything. She opened the cabinet and got down the mugs and put them on the tray.

"Nancy?"

"If nobody else wants it, I'll take the whiskey," Nancy said. She looked at the two men. "That's allowed, isn't it? I mean, with you two on duty and all. Just some ice, Glory."

"It's allowed," the sergeant said. "Most definitely. In fact, I wish we could join you. But please go right ahead."

She put all the things on the tray. Then she poured a glass of the red wine for herself. She carried the tray in and put it down and went around to the other side of the coffee table and sat down on the floor, facing him. She picked up the wineglass by the stem and held it with both hands up close to her forehead, looking at him from around the bowl part.

"Okay," she said. "Go ahead."

"Well," the sergeant said, "we hate to barge in on you like this, and we really won't take up much of your time. The reason we're here is that maybe you might be able to help us and we'd like to ask a few quick questions. As the doorman told you, at least, I hope he told you, we're just sort of visiting the tenants in this building whose apartments face the front here. Where you can look down to the street. And that's about it, I guess. We've just been upstairs talking to Mrs.—uh—to Mrs. . . ." He looked over at his partner.

"Cohen," Olsen said. "Mrs. Cohen. Maybe you know her. Just up above you here, facing front like this."

"We don't know anybody here," Gloria said. "And nobody here knows us. Or cares. That's the way it is in New York."

"Well," the sergeant said, "we're asking everybody to help us if they can. As you know, there were two murders in the hotel across the street down there. Nothing to worry about, now. Doesn't affect this building at all. But we're asking people if they can remember seeing anything unusual down there the last couple of days or so. We haven't got very much to go on and—"

"Jack the *Ripper*," Nancy said. "Boy, you don't think I look all around me, and up and down, when I'm walking down this street?"

The sergeant smiled at her. "Well, I don't think there's any cause for that much alarm. And as for Jack the Ripper, well, that part is really pretty hoked-up."

"Listen," Nancy said, "the *Daily News* has got a guy slinking all over this part of town in a black cape and stuff. Maybe even a red satin lining. I think he stands in doorways a lot."

"Have you ever seen anybody down there in a black cape?" Olsen said.

"No. Not really."

"I know," he said. "Me neither."

The sergeant put the mug down and lit another cigarette. "Okay, I think we can scratch the black capes. But have either one of you noticed anything unusual otherwise? Say, looking out the window?"

"I never look out the window," Gloria said.

"Okay. How about any time you were entering or leaving this building? Ever happen to see anybody strange coming in or going out of that hotel down there?"

"No, not really. Lot of strange-looking folks in this neighborhood anyway. Lord, I don't know what anybody'd have to do to get someone to pay any special notice to them."

He nodded. "All neighborhoods. You should see mine, where I live. People walk around on their knuckles. That's one of the things that makes these cases so hard to work on."

"Is there any more of that whiskey?" Nancy said. "No, no. I'll get it. Listen, the *Daily News* is talking about a mad, crazy surgeon and things like that. You know. What do they call them? Scalpels and things. Can I get you some more coffee while I'm up?"

The sergeant shook his head. "No, thanks. Still have some here. And I know. I *have* to read all that newspaper stuff as part of my job. In fact, I guess as much as anything, that's one of the reasons why we're here. To tell you not to worry about all the wild things you might read about this. People read these stories, see it on television, and they start to get frightened. But it isn't Jack the Ripper and nobody is standing around in doorways waiting to pounce out at you. It doesn't work that way in real life. It's just two pimps . . . uh, excuse me, ladies; it's just these two men killed in a run-down hotel. That's about as exciting as it gets. No more. See? That make you feel better?"

"Oh, sure," Gloria said. "Lots."

"No, really. You two girls living alone. Mrs. Cohen upstairs. Well, we have men going around all the time, and the fact that the murders occurred down there doesn't make this area any less safe than anyplace else, really."

"Besides," Olsen said, "what the *News* hasn't faced up to with their mad-surgeon angle is that you can't ever get a doctor to make a house call anymore."

Gloria blinked at him.

"You know: house call," he said. "Uh, doctor. Surgeon. And, uh . . . Well, forget it."

She put the wineglass down on the table. Then she looked up and smiled, first at Olsen, then at the sergeant. And she relaxed the muscles across her back and shook her shoulders a bit. Everything was going to be fine now.

"But what are we supposed to look for?" she said.

"That's it. You don't *look* for anything; that's too defeating. Everybody pretty much sees the same things every day as they go in and out. You get so that you don't really see them, in effect. It's the unusual thing you might have noticed, that you perhaps remarked on at the time and then forgot all about. Does that make sense?"

Gloria nodded back at him. "You know," she said, "you have sort of dimples."

"I have . . . hmmm?"

"There," she said. "On each side. Not so much when you smile, but just when you're talking like that. Maybe not real dimples, but those two lines right there, in your cheeks. You know what we used to say in Oklahoma about how you got dimples?"

He blinked.

"We used to say that they came from drinking moonshine out of Mason home-canning jars."

"Really?"

"Oh, man," Olsen said, "I could listen to that soft accent all night. That is some kind of voice, lady."

"Gloria," she said.

The sergeant held up his hand. "Uh, anyway," he said, "anyway, if you could give us any help at all, we would be most grateful."

Nancy sat down again and swirled the ice around in her glass. "We saw the pimp car," she said.

"You mean the Lincoln Continental? All tricked up?"

"Uh huh. Mirrors and things. You know. Aerials."

"Very good. Now you're thinking, see? The lady upstairs, Mrs. Cohen, also saw the car and told us about it. Every little bit helps here. Incidentally, we have the car. Or we *had* it; the finance company has gotten it back now."

"And we saw the *pimp*," Nancy said. "How about that? Well, it was *a* pimp, anyway. Now, I don't know if he was one of the ones killed down there or not."

"Maybe the ones who were killed weren't the man we saw," Gloria said. "In fact, I don't really think so."

"And a *girl*, too," Nancy said. "Boy, I'm getting good at this. We saw one of the hotel hookers there. Dirty little old thing. Yuck."

The sergeant looked at them both. Then he tilted his mug over and looked down into it. "You know," he said, "if it wouldn't be too much trouble, maybe I *will* have just a dash more coffee. If there's any left."

"I'll get it," Gloria said. She uncrossed her legs and stood up. She looked down at him. "It was just a little girl we saw. Young."

"Mmmm hmmm. She's probably back in Westchester by now, or whatever. They're usually runaways at that age. Did you ever see any of her customers?"

"No. I think she was just getting started."

"Any strange guys hanging around the hotel?" Olsen said.

She looked back in from the stove. "You already asked that."

"Oh? I guess it's just because I want to hear you talk some more. 'Yawl reddy ast that.' Man."

"I have an accent, too, you know," Nancy said. "Well, maybe not as much; I've been working to get rid of mine since I've been here. But still, some folks say that an Oklahoma accent, you know, goes better with a littler girl like me. Don't you think?"

Olsen nodded. "Yes, ma'am," he said.

The sergeant came into the kitchen. "Just a little bit," he said. "That's plenty, thanks. This is very good coffee; I drink about eighty cups of this stuff a day. Keeps me going, but it's blowing my stomach."

"You ought to take better care of yourself," Gloria said.

"You're too skinny, for one thing. Your wife should see to it that you—"

"Single," he said. "I was married; not now. What's that perfume you're wearing?"

"What perfume?"

He leaned forward and breathed in again. "I don't know. Whatever it is."

"Oh, I don't know. I never do. It's something. Belongs to Nancy; I never look at the labels. I just put it on and take off."

He nodded. "You know, you're almost as tall as I am. You're tall for a girl. See?"

"Mmmm hmmm."

"And you look like you take a lot better care of yourself than I do. Uh, wait. I don't want that to sound wrong. You know. What I mean is, you seem to, well . . ."

"I know," she said. "Well, that's all the coffee."

"Uh, right. Yes. Well, listen, you've both been very helpful and we appreciate it. I hope we haven't taken up too much of your time."

"No, no. I feel better now."

"Better?"

She blinked at him. "Well, I mean not scared anymore."

"That's good. And thanks for your help again."

"We really didn't tell you anything, I guess. You know, aren't you pretty young to be a detective? Is a detective sergeant better than a detective, regular?"

"One grade up. You take a civil-service test. A regular detective is a police officer who has been assigned."

"Oh. But you are all supposed to be fat old guys. They go around with a wooden kitchen match in their teeth."

"Only in movies. And I know you won't believe this but I don't even own a snap-brim hat." He turned and looked over his shoulder. "Come on, Harv."

Olsen was standing at the window, looking down. He turned. "You can see the hotel real good from here," he said. "But very few guys down there in capes."

"You look in the doorways?" Nancy said.

"Come on," the sergeant said. "And thanks again for taking the time to talk to us. And the wonderful coffee." He stopped at the door and looked back at them. "And, remember now, please don't worry about the neighborhood. Or the stories in the papers. We've got this area well covered, as I said. You'll both be fine."

"Here's our card," Olsen said. "Third Homicide Zone, it's right on here. Phone number. Just call either one of us any time if you see anything. In fact, call if you don't see anything. Just call and chat."

"Goodbye," Gloria said.

She relocked everything.

"That tall, thin one was *dynamite*," Nancy said. "Jesus, I could take off my clothes and get up and roll around in his hair when it's like that."

"I don't think I should have mentioned the dimples," Gloria said.

"Well, it did sort of shake him up. But what the hell."

"They weren't really dimples so much as—"

"I know what you mean. You know, I just thought, maybe we ought to have told them that we met the little bitty hooker; you know, that you talked to her?"

Gloria yawned, arms up over her head. Then she locked all her fingers together and pulled down on an imaginary weight. "Naw, I don't suppose so. Not important anyway. The sergeant said that she's probably back home by now anyway, so it wouldn't make any difference, right?"

"I guess not. Anyway, I bet he asks you out."

"Who?"

"Who? The detective *sergeant*, dummy. You think I'm talking about the other one?"

"Out?"

"Well, certainly, out. I'll just bet that he comes around again just to ask if you've seen anything new or something dumb like that. And all he really wants is to stand there and look at you a lot. If you had gotten up and down from the coffee table about one more time in that blouse, I swear he would have poured his coffee into his ear, for God's sake."

"You're just seeing things that aren't there."

Nancy poured the last of the whiskey. "Tell me those boobs aren't there."

Gloria looked down at herself. Then she shook her shoulders a little bit and watched the swaying, soft wiggle. "Well, it's the week before my period."

"You know that. And I know that. But what does a police sergeant know from periods? All he can see is big tits."

"Maybe. Anyway, who cares? I'm going to go to bed."

"I'm going to finish this drink first. See what's on television. Good night."

"Night."

She closed the door and listened for a moment until she heard Nancy turn on the television. Then she went to the closet and reached up to the top shelf and pulled the small suitcase down. She put it on the bed and unzipped it and got out the black leather case.

She sat on the edge of the bed and looked at the razors. She lifted out the Tuesday one and got it just right in her palm and then rolled her hand over to open it. She licked her left thumb with the tip of her tongue and then drew the thumb lightly across the edge of the blade. She bent over under the reading lamp and looked closely at the thumb where the whorled part of the thumbprint came up. There was a tiny, fine line cut through there. She folded the blade closed and put the razor back into its black velvet slot and looked at the others.

She lifted out the Wednesday one and balanced it in her palm. Then she gripped it tightly and rolled her hand over the same way as before. She shook her head no. She put it back and took out the Tuesday razor again, then stood and slipped it into her pocket. She snapped the monogrammed case closed and put it to one side, then zipped the suitcase shut and put it back up on the shelf.

Nancy was on the floor, on her stomach, watching the television, when Gloria came out of the bedroom.

"I forgot about the garbage," she said.

Nancy didn't look around. "Your turn," she said.

Gloria turned back and picked up the leather case from the bed and carried it into the kitchen. She pulled the garbage sack out from under the sink and reached over and got out one of the green plastic bags from the junk drawer. She searched around in the garbage until she found the empty half-gallon milk carton and she carefully ripped open the top. She slipped the flat leather case into the carton and then tucked the top back together where it folded inward. She put the carton into the plastic bag and then shook the rest of the sack of garbage down over it.

She twisted the little green fastener around the top of the plastic bag and then picked up the bag.

"Be right back," she said.

"Big deal," Nancy said. "So how long does it take to dump the garbage?"

At the end of the hall, she pulled back on the pull-down door to the incinerator chute and stuffed the whole thing in. Then she gave it a little shove and listened to it fall, rattling off the sides. And, brushing the palms of her hands together, she went back to the apartment.

seventeen

HE CAME BACK from the deli with the containers of coffee and handed them in through the car window. "Here. Hold these just a second. You think the coffee was bad up there in that last apartment we were, wait till you taste this." He went around to the driver's side, opened the door and got in. "So, okay." He took one of the cups. "So what do you think?"

The sergeant worked on the lid of his coffee, bending forward and holding the styrofoam cup between his open knees, prying up with his thumb and turning the cup slowly in his hands.

"Well," he said. "These goddamn things. They make them so you can't get them off. Well, that last apartment where we were? I must confess that any girl with a set of jugs like that can't be all bad."

"Uh huh. I noticed. What about the other one?"

"What other one?"

"Her roomie," Olsen said. "Come on."

"Mmmm, I don't know. Just another roommate. Where do you put these lids? Any cops around?" He dropped his out the car window. "Look, you see all these buildings down this block? Well, I promise you that every other apartment in every one of these buildings has got a roommate just about like that one we saw just now. No, I'm serious. It's part of the city building code or something like that."

Olsen nodded. "Think maybe those two are dykes? A little fore-and-aft number there?"

"Dykes? No, I'd say not. Christ, Olsen. I told you that you've been married too long. You should be able to recognize a plain, old-fashioned horny look when you see one. I thought the little chunky one up there—uh, Nancy—was going to come right over the table after you. No, what I'm telling you is, it's the old thing again. Women do this to themselves; I think maybe it's something they sneak into their cereal when they're little girls. You ever see two really good-looking women together? No, never. It's not allowed. They don't do it that way. Remember when you had blind dates? Well, the roomie named Nancy up there was always the one you got. She was the one where her friend would say, 'She's a barrel of fun, kid; we laugh all the time.' No, they're probably not dykes. Pre-dyke, maybe."

"Okay. I'll go for that. You mean to tell me that the hefty little bugger was going to throw me down and take it away from me? Christ, I sure didn't catch that act, and I'm old Sam Hard-On. Well, anyway. So what about the other apartments?"

"You tell me."

"We can scratch Mrs. Cohen. And"—he looked at his notebook —"that other old broad—ummm—Brayton. But what about the two queers downstairs just below the girls? So where do they come in?"

"Not allowed to call them queers anymore," the sergeant said. "Departmental stuff. They're called gays now."

"Okay, okay. Scratch the two queer gays. Look, can we go now? You're filling up the car with smoke."

The sergeant cracked the vent-window a bit. "No, hang on. I want to watch their building a little longer."

"You're the boss." Olsen unbuttoned his coat and slouched down, adjusting his gun against the seat. "So tell me again about what we're looking for exactly."

"How would I know? Christ's sake, you're sure right about this coffee. No, okay. Looking for. This is nuts-and-bolts time again. We're just looking is what we're doing. If we haven't got anything, then we check what we *have* got all over again, one more time. And they're pressuring me; you heard the phone call. Well. One: we've got a dead rich pimp and he was done in by a straight-edge razor. Old English, pearl-handled model. And then, suddenly, we have two more dead pimps killed in pretty much the same way. Like a trademark or something. Which leaves us with a guy running around town with his medical bag or all of his pockets full of razors. And all we have to do is find him. And that's it; now you know everything I know."

Olsen shook his head. "You sure that little fat broad was ready to lay me? No, go ahead, DeMario. I'm listening. No, really."

"Well. Check everything again. Who saw who. Whom. Go over all our lists, talk to that doorman again. Who did he see? Who did the people around *here* see? If the cuttings were done in that hotel right over there, there's a possibility that the cutter could live right here in the neighborhood. Chances are better that he's hidden up in Harlem someplace. And he took over the hookers of the dead guys. But we check."

"What about the Mafia? We're still allowed to call them Mafia?"

"No way. Things are tough enough without the old Mafia bullshit. It isn't them. They all have gun fixations; they're probably all as scared of straight-edge razors as anybody else. They don't kill that way. It's too hard to get blood off an Italian-silk suit."

Olsen shrugged. "Fine. Which brings us around to that book you told me."

"The book. Jesus, that's really long-shot time. But, hell. If we're going to look at all possible angles, then we look at that angle, too. It was the *Daily News* that made me think of the book in the first place."

"I know. You said. Chrissakes, DeMario, you tell anybody about that angle and they really pull your chain."

"I know," the sergeant said. "Well, shit. Let's get out of here. This street bores me."

"Okay. I'm about to bust a bladder anyway, that coffee. But, listen, I could come back any time you say and look at big blondie again. Pre-dyke or not. I mean, those are some kind of knockers, right?"

"You'll get a chance to come back, all right. And, yes, granted on the tits. Right now, I don't think there's a lot of doubt about her sexuality. But she's kind of coltish. No, don't look at me like that; it's a perfectly good word. Kind of coltish, if you follow me —as though she really hates being beaten at anything. And she's pretty goddamn cool for being a hick. Young hick, at that. There's no sense of rube in her. Probably she's always been cool like that, since she was a kid. She just looks at you very steadily without blinking."

"Big ball-breaker is what."

"Christ, Harv, all women are ball-breakers. That's also part of the deal with women. But this one here, this Gloria, would also be sensational in bed. At least in the early going, just based on her basic equipment alone. The *body* could handle it all alone at first. It's all there. No, it's the *closing* part that's always bad with women like her. That's when you've given it your very best shot; the whole routine. All your best moves. And you're all through and you're very proud of yourself, and she looks up at you and says something like 'That's it?' You know."

"God, I wish I knew," Olsen said.

"Anyway, now—"

"You know something?" Olsen said.

"—now, we . . . Uh, what?"

"You look better, DeMario. No, I mean, you got some color in your face or something. You don't look all down. Like bored, even."

The sergeant looked across at him. "Who said I was bored?"

"Well, nobody exactly said it. But I figured."

"Well, I'm not. I feel fine. Almost good. Ready to roll."

"Okay. Now what?"

"Okay, then. Now you get a complete make on both the girls. And the two fairies. Gays. Right? And you go back tomorrow and talk to anybody else in the front apartments there. If your make turns up anything at all, I may just go for the long shot."

"Boy, you do and it's ass-in-a-sling time."

"I know. You know. In fact, you're going to help."

"You mean to tell me that we will—"

"No. Never say it out loud. First, I don't know if we'll have to do it. But if we do, don't say it. Just set it up and we do it."

eighteen ▬▬▬▬▬▬▬▬▬▬

SHE WENT INTO THE PARK at 86th and Fifth Avenue, walking fast past the long bench. The only one there was the youngish drunk again. He was sitting all splayfooted, with his forearms on his knees and his head hanging down. He was spitting down between his feet. She went up the stairs to the black gravelly surface and stood for a few minutes, shifting her weight and shaking each leg to loosen her thigh muscles. Then she began to run.

The reservoir lay to her left behind the chain link fencing. The path was one and one-half miles around. She started out slowly, easing up to a jog, working her shoulders back and forth and rolling her head around to stretch her neck, taking in air through her nose and chuffing it out her mouth. Just about halfway around she leaned forward a little more and picked up the pace. And gradually, she fell into a steady rhythm, so she could just listen to her feet and think.

All. Right. Then. It had been four days now since the police and that part was all over. Everything was clear, in fact. The trash had gone away to wherever they take the trash, probably burning in a garbage dump somewhere out on the edge of the island, maybe. There would be a big, steel-gray cloud hanging over the whole thing, sea gulls flying in and out of it. All the razors would be melted and gummy now. There was only the last one here, in the right front pocket of her warm-up pants. She could feel it every time her right leg came up; it fitted diagonally into the crease between her thigh and where the elastic leg of her panties came down and went under. And when she took off her clothes to shower after running, it would be warm to the touch.

She pulled right slightly to pass another runner, keeping her head down, and then glanced over to make sure that it wasn't Robert Redford. He wasn't even close. It never was Robert Redford anyway, even though they all said that he ran around the reservoir every day when he was in town. Or it could sometimes be a lot of people famous. Actors. Television people. But all you were supposed to do was to maybe nod anyway.

Pick. It. Up. More. And now they had a man in a tan kind of twill topcoat standing on her corner down by the deli every day. He was so obviously a policeman that they had even started nodding at each other every time she walked by. She would nod at him and he would nod at her and smile; his front top teeth needed fixing. But he was there to look after their block as the sergeant had promised, and now she wouldn't have to do it and she could get her life going.

She stayed in the center of the path, listening to the crunching of her feet. Once around.

There was only Barry to worry about now, really. And the last time . . . when? Night before last. Well, that time would have worked out, except . . .

Pick. It. Up. More.

"Let me know if you ever get your mind and body all coordinated," he had said. "In fact, I insist that you call me at any hour of the day or night. It isn't so much going unfulfilled like this. It's just that I'm wearing my clothes out getting in and out of them."

Well, now that everything else was all over, she would take care of *that*. Poor Barry; he must be getting punchy. Well, probably he went home every time and played with himself to work it off. But if she could ever get it timed just right—that one just-right moment when she felt the big surge of love—she would just flat grab him and pull him up inside of her until all the wind came out of him. Get the backs of her heels up against his fat bare fanny and push with them; grab him up under both arms with her hands and pull him up hard, and then lock him into that position and hold him, neither one of them moving. She would bite him with her womb.

She passed the other runner again; he was slowing badly and his face was getting blotchy. Up ahead, a man in railroad-type coveralls was standing watching them, and he waved as she came pounding past, as though it were a race. She nodded at him.

All. Right. Go. Next time, she would fix the backlighting in the apartment for sure, leaving the bathroom door just a little bit open. Or . . . no. She would get one of the patterned Vera top sheets from the twin bed and wrap it all around herself, around her shoulders, holding it closed in front like this. And then she could whip it open like a cape and let him look at all of her at once. Like Wonder Woman, maybe.

Funny, she hadn't thought of that in years now. When she had been a kid, she had run around the half-mile cinder track at the school in her Wonder Woman suit that Mother had made, the muslin sheeting streaming out behind and snapping in the cross wind that always blew across the track there in Greer. She would run, loping along, and wave up at the empty green wooden bleachers with the white stenciled seating numbers. Well, until the older kids had laughed her right out of the place when they came in to practice.

Still, it had helped her win at track when she got into high school, gawky or not. She would run the anchor leg on the 400-meter relay, carrying the baton—her head back, spit coming out of both sides of her mouth—straining hard and hearing the pounding of her feet. And she could see herself in the black glossy boots that seemed to be painted right on, coming up to make a point right over each kneecap. And the little pants that fit like the bottom of her tank suit, and the billowy cape snapping away. But best of all was the mask, with the slit openings for her eyes and coming down into that point across the tip of her nose, fitting tight across her cheeks so that nobody could really tell who she was—just that she was somebody all shiny saving the school.

She passed the man in the railroad coveralls again; he was standing by the big bush, grinning and looking approvingly at her. "Run good," he said, or something like that, but she lost his voice in the wind. The other runner on the path with her must have quit. Or died. Around again.

She had the rhythm now and the hurting eased just inside her chest where each rack of ribs came up and joined together. Now she was striding, hammering along smoothly and burning up everything. All the fantail shrimp, this morning's blueberry-cheese

sweet roll. All right, they're called Danish. These dumb East-
erners anyway. But whatever, she was burning it off. All the
runners she knew reached this state. The marathoners all said
that after it stopped hurting a lot, they got into this floaty stage
where their sugar and their blood got all in balance and they
could hold the pace for miles, not thinking about running, just
daydreaming to the beat of it.

Go, Wonder Woman. Two. More. Laps. She was breaking the
sweat now, all beading across her upper lip and inside the
warm-ups, and the front of her hair was pasted down alongside
her temples.

The police sergeant had been nice. DeMario. No problem with
him. When he had come into the kitchen to stand up close and
tell her how good the coffee was, she had felt the mannish part
of him, the—uh—what? The off-duty part, warming his face.
Fine. And she had gotten a flash of it right down *there*. Maybe it
had been the way she was standing, leaning against the kitchen
counter with her legs crossed in the tight pants. But whatever. It
had been a sure-enough attraction. Sometimes it happened to
you; not often. It was like when a man and a woman were just
talking, their *things* were sort of straining toward each other.
Well, being attracted certainly couldn't hurt anything. The thing
was, he would go on to other stuff; he would have to. New York
couldn't hold onto any one subject because events go by too
quickly in New York. Which is why these things work. And now
she could get back . . .

She came up to the railroad man again and glanced over at
him. He made a quickish little move with his hands and she saw
that he had his penis out. It was hanging down, out of the
striped pants, and it was all sort of violet on the end like a rash.
She looked away, slamming ahead past him.

Christ, all *mighty*. Goddamn. She could feel the sudden flush
burning in her neck, swelling up to both sides of her cheeks. She
put her head down and picked it up a beat, driving forward
along the path. *Shit*. Wasn't there *any*place? She glanced back
over her shoulder, then looked ahead. She looked over past the
steps down to the long bench as she pounded past. It was empty
now. Wouldn't there be any other *runners*, for God's sake? Anybody? They had told her about this. She was really sweating
harder now, running cold down under her arms and the backs of
her thighs. God*damn* all this. That girl at work, Janie, she had

been flashed by a man on the subway; Janie had been sitting down and the man had been hanging onto one of the overhead handles. And he had taken it out and pushed it right up close to her face. To her *face*. What did . . .

"I looked away," Janie had said. "I looked away and I slid over to one side and I got off at the next stop."

Well, *shit*. What was *happening* to everybody? Slid over to one side. Why? Everybody had told her about all this; all the stories told over lunch and down in the Time-Life Building cafeteria. Don't go into the park after dark, they had told her. All right, that made sense; fair enough. But don't do *any*thing. Don't run around the reservoir when it's even halfway close to dark. Try not to run alone if you can help it. All right, too. Where are you now, Robert Redford? Where?

She angled slightly to the outside of the path coming around toward the big bush, watching for him. He was still there. He was watching for her. She pounded closer, looking over at him.

He was masturbating now, half crouched, with his legs far apart and his hips thrust forward, pointing it at her. Pumping his hand fast, with the violet tip sliding in and out.

She slammed to a stop, jolting, hurting both heels, and spun around. "Stop it," she said.

He shuffled a few steps forward, legs still apart, his right hand going up and down faster. The other hand was out away from his body, fingers all apart. There was a circle of spit around the edges of his mouth.

She took a quick breath and moved toward him. "I said to stop it," she said.

He was looking into her eyes. And he was blinking. "I'm fucking you now," he whispered. He sped up the motion of his hand. The reddish tip flashed in and out. "I'm fucking you now, fucking you now, fucking . . ."

The first spurt of semen came all at once and it landed on the left knee of her warm-up pants. Then there was another, a smaller one, that fell on the edge of the path, all plopped out like yellowish phlegm.

She aimed as if she were kicking a field goal: one little short step and she swung her foot up hard, both arms all the way out for balance, driving the toe of her Adidas running shoe right up into the middle of him. The shock stung all up the front of her shinbone, jarring hard.

He went over backward, both arms out, glancing off the bush, then came back doubled over forward. The next kick caught him in the left ear and he slid down sideways and pulled his knees up against his chest.

She stood there, panting hard. Her hair was stuck down to the sides of her face so that she had to pull it away from her cheeks. She swung her right hand down and pulled the zipper halfway down on the pocket of her warm-up pants. Then she zippered it closed again.

"Goddamn you," she said. "You son of a bitch. I told you *stop* it, I said. I ought to kill you for this. Cut your fucking *heart* out. Doesn't anybody around here do anything about all this? Anybody?"

He was lying on his side in the grass, all doubled, still looking up at her. His mouth was even wetter. "Again," he said, whispering it. "Kick me again. More and more. Kick me here. Right here."

Oh, *God.* She turned and ran.

She walked fast to the apartment, head down, looking at the wet stain on her knee every time the leg moved forward. The wind cutting across the intersections made her clammy; the inside of the sweat shirt was sticking to her stomach and across her shoulders in back.

She didn't nod at the policeman in the tan twill topcoat on the corner, and she swung in past the doorman, scowling. In the elevator, she jabbed her thumb at the number Five, fishing in her left front pocket for the keys.

And Nancy began opening the door from the other side while Gloria was fumbling with the lower lock. "I thought you'd never get home," she said.

"Now what?"

"We've been *robbed,* is what. Just *look.* Look around."

The whole apartment had been tossed around in a jumble. All the canisters were on the kitchen floor, tops off and flour and sugar all spilled out. The cushions were off the couch. The drawers had been pulled out of the hutch and dumped upside down on the floor.

She unzipped the warm-up pants down the side of one leg and shook that leg free; then she unzipped the other leg and let them fall. She stepped out of the pants and then tugged at her panties in the seat where they were sticking wetly up in the crack. "God*damn* it," she said. "When did all this happen?"

"Today. Sometime today. I don't know," Nancy said. "Look at all this."

"What did they get?"

Nancy walked around, pushing at things with one toe. "I don't know; Lord, I can't tell a thing yet. Nothing, as far as I can see so far. Well, the liquor money from the teapot on the floor there, but that wasn't even eleven dollars yet. And I can't find my cassette tape player. You should see the *bed*rooms. Go look. Someone cut the pillows apart, even."

Gloria bent and picked up the warm-up pants, taking care not to touch the stained knee. She carried them into the bedroom.

Her closet was all twisted around. Both suitcases were on the floor, unzipped and open, and the satiny linings were all ripped out. She pulled off her sweat shirt and threw it down hard and then reached around in back and unhooked the brassiere and peeled it away from her breasts where it was still sticking. She stooped and got her robe from the floor and shrugged into it. Shit, oh, dear.

"The bathroom too?" she said.

Nancy came to the door and looked in. "Hell, yes, the bathroom too. It's all on the floor in there. What isn't thrown into the sink and broken. Even the lid is off the tank; you know, where it flushes."

"Well, how did they get in here?"

"I don't know. The door, of course. No marks, no nothing. I just unlocked everything and came in and here it was."

Gloria turned and looked at the rest of it. All her clean underwear was strung out in a trail between the dresser and the bed. Some of the panties had been turned inside out so that the cottony crotches showed against the rayon patterns. Christ.

"Well, I've got to shower first," she said. "I'm all crappy. I don't care what, first I've got to get clean again."

When Nancy left, she picked up the warm-up pants and unzipped the right front pocket and took out the razor and slipped it into her robe pocket. Then she wadded the warm-ups into a ball and walked back into the front room with them. She opened the front door and walked down to the end of the hallway to the incinerator chute. She dropped the pants in and listened to them fall. Then she went back.

"My forty dollars," Nancy said. "The two twenties I had under my mattress; they were even pushed under toward the center, but they found them. And the tape recorder; they got that too. Lord, that looks like about all. Listen, can't you help me here first?"

Christ on a crutch. "I *told* you," Gloria said. "I told you I'm *dirty*. In a *minute*, all right?"

"All right, all right. Go ahead, for God's sake. Jesus, we might as well all shower. Go to the goddamn *dance*. This whole dumb town is a madhouse anyway. Where are our cops now, huh? 'We have men in the neighborhood.' My *ass*. 'Don't worry about anything, girls.' Shit. Look at all this. Look."

When Gloria closed the bathroom door, Nancy was sitting on the floor and she was crying.

All right, then. All RIGHT, by God. All you dirty, filthy bastards. Somebody *pays*.

Gloria got the shower just as hot as she could take it and, bending under it, letting it pound against her back, she took the complexion brush and scrubbed at her left knee until it grew bright red, the blood close to the surface.

nineteen

ALL RIGHT, buggers. It's justice time. She waited across the street on Eighth Avenue, standing on the sidewalk by the Cadillac, watching the doorway to the café. That was the place, all right: between 54th and 55th. She had read about it in an old copy of *New York Magazine* at the dentist's. The story had said how they all gathered in there to drink and to show off their trick clothes and their diamond rings and to talk big to one another about all the girls they had. They spent whole evenings in there —what was the word?—jiving, while their women were out hustling. All right, then. She checked her watch again. It was 2:20 A.M. She looked around both ways on the sidewalk. And then she backed into a doorway where it was darkest, leaning against the brick wall, watching.

Two came out. Wide-brim hats and the fitted full-length topcoats, all nipped in close at the waist. They stood there for a moment, talking, and then they slapped palms. The smaller one headed down toward 55th, his heels clicking it off. The other one came toward her, tugging on a pair of light-beige gloves. He was whistling.

She put her hand into her raincoat pocket and touched the razor.

He pulled out a ring of keys, shook them around to find the right one, and leaned over and unlocked the car door. Then he reached in and lifted the car telephone out of its cradle and stood up again, the phone line curling in little white circles going back inside the car. He leaned against the roof with one forearm, said something into the phone and then waited.

She took her right hand out of her pocket and rolled it over smoothly, then held the open razor down close to the side of her leg.

His voice drifted back across the sidewalk. "Hey, baby," he said into the phone, "what's goin' down?" He shifted his weight and crossed his legs, chuckling.

She took three fast steps toward him, tensing her arm, leading slightly with her left shoulder.

Then, suddenly, he doubled over, laughing into the phone. She checked the big swing halfway through, bumping it off his bent elbow. He straightened, looking at her in surprise.

"Hey," he said. "Hey, you drunk or something? Man, get *off* of me. You hear?"

She went back a step, swinging her right hand down behind her thigh again. "Excuse me," she said.

"Drunks," he said, still holding the phone. "Go 'wan, now. Get out of here or I'm gonna kick your big white ass. Go 'wan."

She nodded. And then she turned and walked away.

twenty

"KEEP YOUR VOICE DOWN," the sergeant said.

Olsen leaned over closer, his palms on the desk. "Sorry. What I was *saying* was, how'd you like that little number I did with her underpants? You know, turning a few of them inside out there, like maybe it was a sex fiend did it? I mean, I didn't exactly bite out the crotches or anything, but it wasn't bad."

"I saw. Not a bad touch. I'm only sorry nothing else turned out. That's a lot of work, you know?"

"Do I. Listen, what do we do with their money? The little tape recorder?"

"Well, put the money in an envelope and . . . What is it? Forty dollars? And slip it into the Benevolent Fund; make it anonymous. And you're a good cop again. I don't know about the tape recorder; I'll think of something."

Olsen nodded. "You figure we really had to take stuff?"

"I told you. You steal something and it's a burglary. If you don't take anything, it looks like a search. Jesus, I don't know. Maybe I should have made you chew up her underwear; it would have served you right."

"Come on. So where are we now?"

"Back where we started." The sergeant pushed at the papers on the desk until he found the report. "Well, it was almost worth the try, I guess. You hit on one of these things and you win the whole pot. I mean, look at this, see? Gloria-Ann Cooper. Twenty; almost twenty-one. Big and healthy girl. Perfectly clean. True blue. But she came to town just four days before our first cutting, see? That's one. All right. Oklahoma City to Chicago. Chicago to Newark. Newark bus to the Port Authority. Fine. Now, then. Now we have Nancy Marie Cavanaugh. Twenty-three. Also a good kid. Same hometown; first cousins. And—"

"When I do a run-up on somebody, I do a run-up," Olsen said.

"You do, indeed. Now. When Girl A arrives in town, Girl B is over at Harkness Pavilion, having had the shit kicked out of her in a mugging. Welcome to New York. Okay. So Nancy Cavanaugh is in bed over there for two and a half of the four days. And do any of the nurses you talked to recall her being visited by Gloria-Ann Cooper? They're not sure, but they don't think so."

"Couple of visitors came over from *Time* magazine," Olsen said. "But the nurses couldn't remember any big blondes. That's pretty ragged information, though. I wouldn't . . ."

The sergeant nodded. "I know. And I'll give you that one. But, still, wouldn't it be sort of strange if Gloria hadn't rushed right over to see Nancy? Just arriving in town to hear such shocking news and all that? Where was Gloria? Sitting in the apartment?"

"Well, hell. You could always up and ask her, you know."

"No, you *can't*, Harv. Jesus Christ. You ask her why she didn't visit Nancy and she simply looks at you without blinking, icy-cool, and says, 'I can't stand the sight of blood,' or something like that. And there you stand with your fly open, meathead. No. But, what the hell. All this part is getting too thin anyway. Now, where was I? Okay. Look at this, see here? Victim One was a pimp. Even if he was rich and fancy. And a lot of pimps work the terminal over there. I'll admit that's a reach, but the thing is, this one could have. I don't know, maybe I shouldn't have read that goddamn book. But anyway, down he goes and out go Grampa's razors. Now. We still can't find out who was at the party up at his apartment, and chances are we never will. I wouldn't tell, either, if it was me. We'll simply never know; those people are long gone. But you talked to the doorman and got a rundown on who came out of there. Could be anybody. But there are two big girls on the list, along with everybody else, right?"

"Right. One of them carrying two suitcases."

"A lot of people carry suitcases in New York. But, sure. And I found an evening gown up there that just might fit a big girl; it was red, soft stuff. Christ, if it *was* Gloria, I'd give my left front fender to see her wedged into that thing, everything sort of hanging out. Anyway—"

Olsen drummed his fingers on the desk. "Cut low in front?"

"Huh? Yes, yes. Come on, for Christ's sake. Anyway, Victims Two and Three get it right across the street from where the girls live. And the two fags, too, for that matter. We haven't cleared them yet, either. Same style, same weapon, we think. So what can we do as decent, law-abiding citizens? We go in and toss their apartment. And what do we find? Nothing."

"Her purse was on the dresser there," Olsen said. "I looked in it; the lining, everything. You think she could have carried them while running at the reservoir?"

"I don't think so. You saw her leave for the park; all she was wearing was a sweat shirt and warm-up pants."

"Brassiere under there. I didn't think she owned any."

"Jesus, Harv. A pair of tits like that and you're supposed to wear a brassiere to run in. You could shake the park apart. But the thing is, what have we got?"

"No case," Olsen said.

twenty-one

LORD, she'd have to stop shivering like this. The dumb doorway wasn't any protection at all; the rain was pounding in slantwise and getting in under her jacket collar and running cold down the front of her neck. And the boots weren't any good like the salesman had promised. Even her sweat socks were wet now. She curled her toes down. And with her right hand, she held hard to the razor, watching him.

He was sitting in the car, the engine running and all the windows up, talking on the phone again. The rain was bouncing high off the roof, making a halo around the top of the car, and the water was running in sluices down the sides. The window on the driver's side had a lumpy section of fog rising up from the inside so that he looked all shadowy and out of focus. It was 3:15 A.M. The streets were clear.

All right, then; time to pay. You got away once. But not again. You had better be talking to God on that phone.

She stepped out of the doorway and across the sidewalk quickly. She leaned over and rapped on the window with the knuckles of her left hand. She could see him look around at her, squinting. She rapped again. He turned his face away from the telephone and reached over and pushed the button. The window came down about two inches and stopped.

She put her mouth up close to the opening and spoke low.

"What?" he said.

"I'm cold," she said. "Help me."

He brought the window down a few more inches and leaned over closer. "What you sayin'? I can't hear you."

Low again: "I'm cold, sweet honey-man. Help me."

The window came all the way down now. "Who are you workin' for, sugah?" he said.

She feinted left and brought her right hand around in a backhand, rolling the wrist over fast. The blade glanced off his chinbone, tearing away a flap of skin, and sank into his neck just under his right ear. She put her shoulder into it hard and pressed down, drawing it across toward her. It slid through the gristle of his Adam's apple, cutting in deep, and she swung it around up into the softer skin on her side.

She pulled the blade away and shook it. Then she reached in through the window and released the door latch, stepped back and opened the door. She stepped around it and reached it for him, getting his lapel in her left hand. He was holding his neck and making a faint humming noise. She could feel the splash of blood sticky on her wrist between her jacket sleeve and the top of her kidskin glove. She pushed.

He went back, jerking, still holding the cream-colored telephone in his right hand. The mouthpiece began filling with blood; it was sinking into all the tiny round holes and then spilling out over the sides.

He coughed suddenly, his eyes wide, and blood came splashing out of his nose and mouth. He was trying to say something, but his mouth kept filling to stop the word. He kicked with both legs, shaking them hard.

She pulled his topcoat to one side, where it overlapped, then got hold of the underside and pulled that back. He sneezed up a burst of blood against her hair and forehead.

She tore his sport coat open, popping off the one big pearly button and leaned up over him. She placed the blade down against his abdomen and slid the blunt tip of it up underneath his snakeskin belt. And then she pressed down hard, using all her forearm, and drew the blade down between his legs, rising high over him and pressing down hardest at that point, finally bringing it back up to the top of his left thigh. The blood from his throat was starting to spray down across her hair. It began dripping into her right eye. More began to slide off slowly at the end of her nose, falling thick onto the tops of his legs.

"All you sons of bitches," she said.

She backed out and kicked the car door shut. And she straightened and looked around, listening.

Then she stepped back into the darkness of the doorway and held her head back and her hands out, the palms pointed upward. She stood that way for several minutes, until the pounding rain washed all the blood away.

twenty-two

"NICE TALKING TO YOU, Mr. Ripper," the sergeant said. "Now, if you'll excuse me, I—"

"No, *listen* to me. Please." The little man tugged at his black knit necktie again; it was down to where all the top button showed on his shirt collar. "I mean it. I'm really him: Jack the Ripper. I told you already. I told them downstairs at the precinct desk. And they sent me—"

"Excuse me. The phone again," the sergeant said. He picked it up and listened, then nodded. "Yes, yes. Put him through." He covered the mouthpiece with the butt of his hand and looked back at the man sitting beside the desk. "Sorry about all these calls. Now, then. What did you say you killed them all with?"

The man patted at all the pockets on his coat. "Oh, here," he said. He reached into the left inside pocket and pulled out a knife. It had a dirty wooden handle and a serrated blade. "See?" He shifted his grip and grabbed the knife dagger style, the blade down. "I stabbed and cut and *hacked* them, see?" He leaned across the desk and waved the knife in a circular motion over the papers.

The sergeant nodded, watching. Then he took a quick breath and said, "Olsen!" He looked at the man again. "Put it down. *Down.*" He pulled his hand away from the mouthpiece of the phone and spoke into it. "Be with you in a minute, lieutenant. No. A *minute.*" He looked back at the serrated blade. "Will you put down that fucking *knife*, I said. Olsen!"

"Oh, Jesus," Olsen said.

"Oh, Jesus, your ass. Will you get this crazy son of a bitch out of here before he *cuts* somebody? Out. Somebody do something."

The man stood twisting and kicking under Olsen's hands. "I said I want to confess and take my punishment. I want to get square with God, don't you understand?"

"Well, get in line." The sergeant turned back to the phone, shaking out a cigarette with his free hand. "Yes, sir. Are you feeling any better? Oh? Too bad. Yes, yes, it's every bit what it sounds like here. I know, I know. That's the fourth Jack the Ripper I've talked to this afternoon; the next one is going to come walking in here with a fucking gun and shoot up the place. Don't they stop anybody at the desk down there?"

He leaned forward, shoulders hunched up, listening. "No, none of them are any good," he said. "I also have a deskful of signed confessions here and this last thing happened only this morning. Yes. Yes, of course we'll read them all. No."

He patted at all the papers on the desk until he felt the lighter, then picked it up and lit the cigarette.

"Yes, sir, I do need more help. Thank you. I appreciate that. Yes, I know it's a big city."

Olsen came back and sat down in the chair. He looked over and shrugged.

"But . . . No, pretty much midtown, right here in our zone. I know the area. Uh, next? Well, I don't know if there'll be a next. None of us . . . Yes."

He covered the mouthpiece again and looked at Olsen. "What'd the doc say?"

Olsen looked at the backs of his hands. "Probably razor."

The sergeant turned back to the phone. "Looking for, yes. No, I don't think it's a madman. No, sir. Nice reading in the papers, but no ghoul or . . . Christ, no. What we probably have got on our hands is a full-bore pimp war. Uh, yes, sir. I am busy. But it was nice of you to call. Now, you try and get some rest, all right? I'll keep you posted, yes."

He hung up and put both elbows on the desk and his hands over his face.

"You're a great fucking help to me in my hour of need," he said.

"Sorry," Olsen said. "Won't happen again."

"Okay. What did the report say?"

"Man, that poor sumbitch was some kind of cut up. Jesus. We could start a cock collection down at the morgue."

"Swell."

"Hell, his dong was cut clean—"

"I *saw* him this morning, remember? I know where it was cut. Now, what else?"

"It'll be over in a minute; they're making copies now. You can read it. So what do we do now?"

The sergeant turned his head slightly and looked out at Olsen through his spread fingers.

"I'm glad you asked me that question," he said.

twenty-three

SHE TOOK A SIP of the wine and held it there long enough to let the sparkling part fizz out against her tongue and the roof of her mouth before swallowing, as you do with 7Up. She looked at the three of them, just half listening because they didn't seem to be saying anything important anyway. But just in case, she kept the outside of her face all set in the old stand-away look. That way, if one of them suddenly turned and said something to her directly, she could pause, just right, raise her eyebrows slightly, and say, "Mmmm? Again?"

It put them off every time, the meatheads. When she got it just right, most people would stammer a bit when they had to repeat whatever it was that they had said the first time. She had practiced it ever since she had been small and had discovered the power. It was almost like wearing the mask with the slit eyes and the pointed part coming down over your nose to give you that catlike look. Next to wearing the mask, this was best.

Well, hell. You *had* to do it in order to stay safe. Otherwise, you were just too wide open. If you just let your face stay *regular*, normal, you might as well be dumb-ass Rebecca of Sunnybrook Farm—people could get to you. But this worked. Mother had really hated it, that look, and sometimes used to slap her hard for doing it and yell at her to stop the play-acting all the time. But when she used the special look on Daddy, he used to lean over and squint into her eyes and say, "Are you in there?" And then pat her on the head and wink at her.

Besides, she was feeling just about right: warm toward the

three of them and warm toward everybody in the restaurant. Sort of . . . what? Benign, that was it, like she was looking after all of them and they were all beholden to her, even if they didn't know it. Just like that old-timey portrait of Ethel Barrymore just on your left where you come in past the checkroom. It was a 1906 photograph, with that long neck and icy stare and all; Ethel Barrymore looked as if she were watching over the whole world, too. Hell, she had probably practiced the look, too, and had her picture taken doing it just that way.

"You're very quiet," the sergeant said.

Gloria raised her eyebrows just a bit. "Mmmm?" she said. "Again?"

"All right. Once again: you're very quiet," he said. "More wine?"

"Yes, please. I was just thinking, I guess. Sorry."

She looked at him and his wolfy teeth. They just made him look smart, because he sure as hell wasn't. Sexy, all right, but that didn't matter. She had already stopped worrying about him. Well, not that he had ever been a special threat anyway. Him or anybody in town. The thing is, you have to work up your own priority list of things to worry about. Don't get excited, just work up the list in order of importance. Fine. Number One: What about getting caught? No way, no way. It's clear that the police don't know who they're looking *for,* so how could they ever catch anybody? Fine. Just stay calm at all times, almost as if you had stepped outside of your own body and you were standing over there by the bar, looking back at this table, watching the four people drinking wine. And if you don't have to worry about it, then you just move it down your priority list. Easy as that. You're careful. But you're sure as hell not jumpy.

"I'm really not too good at this," the sergeant said. He tried shaking the bottle over the ice bucket so that the drops would fall back; finally, he wiped the bottom of it with his napkin. "I only have sparkling burgundy about once every five years. Here."

"With us, it's good old Gallo Hearty," Nancy said. "And as long as you're pouring . . ."

The dinner at Gallagher's had really taken shape pretty fast. Gloria had been in the bathtub when the sergeant had called to tell Nancy that he had gotten her tape recorder back. The pawn-shop detail had picked it up and had brought it back to him.

And Nancy had chewed him out a lot about the burglary and no police protection, and the sergeant had said something that took a few minutes, probably that he was sorry. And then Nancy had come to the bathroom door.

"He wants to take us to dinner," she had said. "The sergeant—uh—DeMario, and the other one. Olsen."

"Whatever for?"

"So he can look at *you* some more. I told you. No, he says really that he owes us one after the burglary and all. Even if he did get the tape recorder back. You know."

"Tell him no."

"Already told him yes," Nancy had said. "What's that thing there on your knee? That strawberry spot."

"A little skin scraped; I don't know. Do I have to go?"

"A free meal? You're kidding. At Gallagher's? Course you got to go. And besides, look, you get the single one. I get Olsen, and if he isn't married, I'll kiss your ass until you bark like a fox."

"Well, you don't have to get into bed with him," Gloria had said.

"Not unless he asks."

And now they were all around the table, like old pals, like they had been doing this for years. But all right; it wouldn't matter. Harvey Olsen had ordered the sparkling burgundy to celebrate recovering the tape recorder. He was wearing a coat and pants that matched; he looked a little bit smaller in a suit. She took another sip of the wine and held it in her mouth and looked at Tony DeMario.

His hair was all crispy and stirred around like it had been back in the apartment. And he still had the canning-jar sort of lines running up his cheeks. But the rims of his eyelids were reddish and he looked tired. He saw her watching him and smiled. It converted him quickly into the wolfish look again with those Kelvinator-door teeth. If he bit her, it would really hurt.

"Here's to the tape recorder," he said, and they clinked glasses. "Ummm, tell me, why do you hold the wine in your mouth like that?"

Gloria swallowed. "I like to wear out all the bubbles first. It makes a little white sound in there, a tiny, little fizzy sort of noise that you can hear inside your head."

"Mine gets all the way down to my stomach," Nancy said, "and then it sits down there and gurgles for days."

He leaned across and lit her cigarette, then lit his own. "Anyway, it was very good of you to come to dinner with us."

"I thought that policemen never got any time off," Gloria said.

"Nope, not true. We get days off just like regular people. But it doesn't matter anyway; being a policeman is all fun all the time. It's just one big game of cops and robbers."

"You look tired," she said. "Have you been busy?"

He shrugged. "No more than usual. Normal for this time of year, in fact."

"You ever catch Whatchacallit the Ripper yet?" Nancy said. "I saw in the paper that they've found out it's a whole bunch of razors he's using and not a doctor's thing. Even this last murder the other day. The guy who was killed while he was talking on his car-phone thing."

"Wait a minute," Olsen said. "Hold it. Time. The deal was that we weren't going to talk shop, remember? It's my night off."

Gloria let her face fall back into the look, watching Tony some more. Poor red eyes. He probably needed looking after, too. His poor ribs probably showed all the way up the front. He probably had skinny little old buns.

"Harv is right," the sergeant said. "No shoptalk. We can sit around the office and do that. What I really want to talk about is steak. And spinach salad. The kind they do here with the bacon pieces on top. And the mustard sauce here. I promise you, one taste of this mustard sauce and you're mine for life. Where's the waiter?"

She waited for Tony and Olsen to suggest something, so that she could tell how much money they were ready to spend. It turned out to be the sliced steak with the mustard sauce on the side. They all ordered it.

"And one more wine," Olsen said.

"That's more money on wine than the whole tape recorder was worth," Nancy said. She leaned across and put the very tips of her fingers on his forearm. "But I accept, I accept."

"Our pleasure."

"You like my hair this way?" Nancy said. "I mean, the bangs in front like this?"

Olsen looked at it, nodding slowly. "Sure. It's a . . . a . . . What do you call it? You know what I mean. A pixie."

"Like Mia Farrow," Nancy said. "She's just my size, Mia Farrow."

"But she's too skinny," Olsen said.

"I think so, too."

Gloria let her stomach muscles ease up a little bit more while they ate, all three of them seeming to talk at once. But she kept her toes curled inside her shoes. Tony DeMario was very smooth, if you let yourself forget who he really was for a minute; he had a way of bending his head over his plate and then looking up at her from under his eyebrows. And she really wanted to reach over and pat the palm of her hand across his hair to see what it really felt like. Mostly, she ate steadily, listening to them talk and occasionally nodding or just saying yes or no. When she shifted her weight, she could feel the razor in the right front pocket of the new Sisley jeans.

"Tell me about being libbers," Olsen said.

Nancy looked up at the ceiling and sighed. Then she pointed at her wineglass. Olsen filled it.

"'Libbers,'" she said. "Lord, I shouldn't have ever mentioned anything in the first place. It isn't 'libbers,' Harvey. Or women's libbers. God. I told you in the *cab*, but I guess you weren't listening. Listen, all women are *liberated*, about as much as we're going to get liberated in this century. No. What I said was that I was a member of the organization. I'm a feminist, Harvey. That's all. Not necessarily a *radical* feminist. Well, only radical maybe three days a week. What I am conscious of is rights. I'm aware of what's going down in the world. 'Libbers.' Lord, Harvey."

"Holy smokes, I'm sorry," he said. "Just for that, I'm not going to order you a cigar after dinner."

"You *see?* No, Harv, it's just going to take some time to alter your thinking. But don't you worry your pretty little head about it; we're working on it. And we're making progress. Right, Glory?"

"Not fast enough," Gloria said.

"And that's the way Glory is," Nancy said. "Freedom now or the hell with it. You know, let's *go*, everybody into the trenches. We argue about that a lot."

Gloria shrugged, looking back at the sergeant. Then she took a deep breath. "What about the Ripper?" she said.

He looked up and blinked. Then he smiled. "The—uh—who?"

"Ripper."

He shrugged. "Oh, him. No great thing. He'll turn up."

"What makes you say that?"

"They always do. Especially in things like this. It isn't so much solving these cases as it is a matter of waiting."

"Oh, no you don't," Olsen said. "You guys start talking crime and you're going to screw up my seduction over here, right, Nance?"

Nancy shook her head no. "Jesus, you've still got it all wrong, Harvey. You don't seduce women anymore, Harv. You just flat *ask* them, one human to another. People, Harv. Persons. No advantage taken. Would you care to go to bed with me?"

"Would you?" Olsen said.

"No."

Gloria kept her toes curled inside the shoes. "Why do you say he'll turn up, Tony?"

"Who? Oh, the killer, you mean. Well, it's kind of complicated. You probably wouldn't want to hear it all."

"No, tell me," she said.

"Well, I'll keep it brief, then. See, this isn't just a murder; I mean, there isn't any Agatha *Christie* in this thing. It's spectacular, and that makes all the difference. Shooting somebody is one thing. Or shooting two people, even; people do that. They just haul off and shoot. But here you have a *series* of killings, all of them particularly savage, and all the same technique and style. If style is the word. Well, then. *That's* the part that makes it different, see? You don't hunt for the killer so much as you wait for him to come to you. The very nature of these killings makes it that way."

"I don't follow you at all," Nancy said.

He shifted around in the chair and lit another cigarette. "Okay, look. This is a vendetta against a group of people. In this case, pimps. All right. Not a one-shot, but four murders. It tells us something, right? What it tells us is that a crazed . . . a madman did it who really wants to be caught. A guy who wants to call attention to himself. It's subconscious: he wants to be caught so . . ." He held up one hand, looking at all of them. "No, wait. You'll have to bear with me through this part. Don't look at me like that; I know that this is old-time psychological crap. You get it out of textbooks and all. But, anyway, the *theory* is that he *wants* to be caught to call attention to himself. It would satisfy some weirdo craving. Look, I'm only a detective sergeant and not a Ph.D. But these things happen. It goes on and pretty soon if the guy *hasn't* been caught, he starts to get antsy and he comes to you. He writes you letters; he calls you on the phone. Listen, Jack the Ripper, the real one, did it years ago, in—mmmm—in 1888. The police were busy *not* catching him and finally he started writing them, saying, 'Hey, you guys. I'm over here.' Like that."

God, it's dumb-time again. Gloria didn't realize that she was shaking her head until she noticed him looking at her.

"You don't agree," he said.

"No," she said. "No, but I see what you're getting at. The reason I was shaking my head was that I was trying to think of that old-time movie. You know, where the man took a lipstick and wrote on the mirror. Something about 'stop me,' or something like that. Is that what you mean?"

He nodded. "That's pretty much it. Rough, but yes."

"He'd have a hell of a time today," Nancy said. "First off, where would he find any lipstick today? He'd have to write it on the mirror in chicken fat or something."

"I remember the movie you said, Gloria," Olsen said. "It was *Babes on Broadway*. Ruby Keeler and Dick Whozis. You know."

She looked at all of them, studying their faces. Lord, this was all too easy. It was like looking out through the mask, really. Somebody shiny. "Well, the papers say that you have a confession anyway."

He laughed, looking wolfish again for a flash. "Confession. I'm up to my armpits in confessions. I make Harvey read them all. We even had a Ripper in my office—uh—when? Day before yesterday, and he pulled a knife on me. He kept insisting that he was the guy. Trouble was, it wasn't a good enough knife."

"So how come you know so much about the Ripper?" Nancy said. "No, I don't mean this guy, son of Ripper. I mean Ripper A, the real one."

"Funny you should ask," Olsen said. "Tony just read a whole book about the guy. Word gets out that DeMario read a *book* and they come and take away his badge."

"I really did," the sergeant said. "I don't know, I guess the *Daily News* got me going on the subject with all its stories. So I went over to the library and got it; it's called *When London Walked in Terror* or something like that."

"I stopped at Nancy Drew," Gloria said.

"I know, I know. Everybody did. But just for that, I'll tell you about this one. Can we have some coffee, you think?" He waved for the waiter. "Anyway, it was back in 1888. Big year for murders. There were thirty-five killings in the London home counties, whatever that is, and only eight convictions. I always remember statistics like that; it sounds like the story of my life. So. There was a two million population in East London at the time. You like that? And after the second ripping, they questioned more than one thousand people. And that's it. End of book review."

Gloria nodded. "Okay. But didn't they ever catch him?"

"That's the sad-ending part. The best theory is that he killed five prostitutes in ten weeks and then put rocks in his coat pockets and jumped into the river. The—uh—Thames. He was down three weeks before he finally came up."

"But I thought that everybody knew who he was."

He looked at her and shook his head. "No, not for sure. Everybody had a *theory*. Everybody had his own pet suspect. In fact, Conan Doyle—I guess it was before he became Sir Arthur Conan Doyle—he came up with a *Jill* the Ripper theory. No, really. Conan Doyle lived there at the time and *he* figured that it had to be a *woman* who could move around Whitechapel that way without arousing suspicion with the victims. Or maybe a man dressed up like a woman. They even had a pop song going around London after that. The Jill the Ripper song."

Gloria looked at him closely, holding more wine in her mouth. Poor, tired Tony DeMario. Old ribs and skinny buns. He was looking back at her now with his red-rimmed eyes. The thing was, he would never get it right, just talking about some dumb old book. Jesus, she could probably get the book and underline the passages for him and he wouldn't know where the hell he was. Well, anybody that dumb had it coming. She swallowed. "Well, what about here?"

"Where?"

"Those killings here. In New York City."

"Oh, here. Well, I'm afraid not. First, it looks far too much like a pimp war. Second, if it was a woman, a woman here, I mean, we'd have to start looking for a wronged hooker. But she would be using a gun; they always do. And for every five shots they fire, they blow out three radial tires and maybe hit their guy once in the kneecap. So it wouldn't work here. And, as for a man dressed in women's clothes, what's the big deal about that in New York City? So it's back to the original thing I told you about. We just wait."

She stirred the sugar into her coffee, head down, looking intently at the swirls it was making. This was all so bad. God, nobody can get it right around here. Maybe it was something to do with the town. She put the spoon down on the saucer and raised her head and took a deep breath.

"Well, your original theory is probably all wrong," she said.

He shrugged. "Wouldn't surprise me. They often are. But what's so wrong about it?"

"Well, *really*. I mean, the guilt thing you were talking about a while ago. All that stuff about a madman who wants to get caught, remember? Well, *no*. Suppose it isn't a madman. Or a psychopath; whatever they call those guys. Just suppose that it is a plain *man*-man, that's all. See? You don't have to be a maniac to kill pimps or any really bad people; not if the people have got it coming so bad. No, the killer would be doing a real service. Nobody in New York cares. Who would mourn a pimp? Pimps don't do anything but hurt people. They hurt women really bad. But nobody does anything about that; they're too busy worrying about themselves. All right, so it's a big city and living in the city makes folks numb all over; their feelings, I mean. They see someone hurt, they look the other way. They even cross the street. You could die out there on the sidewalk; you could flat keel over, belly up, and people would come along and step over you, looking the other way on purpose. Fine. So what if it isn't a pimp war or a—uh—what was it you said? A vendetta. What if the killer didn't want to get caught, like you said. Or didn't plan on getting caught, see? Knew he wouldn't be caught. Would he write you any letters or leave you any messages on mirrors? No, siree, he wouldn't. He would just be *doing* it and never look back. Just get it done and get back to work. You know, like—uh—like the mark of Zorro or somebody."

The sergeant was smiling at her again. "All right, all *right*. Put me down. I'm sorry I ever mentioned it in the first place. But what you're proposing, Glory-Ann, is old-time Oklahoma vigilante stuff. Vengeance. Knocking off the sheepherders because they've got it coming."

Oh, Lord. She felt like leaning right over and *biting* him hard. He just flat couldn't get it through his head.

"Oh, I know," she said. "You guys, Nancy here, everybody,

gets me started on this and I get all fired up again. What I *mean* is, I think you're flat wrong in waiting for a crazy man, waiting for him to come to you. It may not be a crazy man like it says in your textbooks or whatever. It's the *city*, see? Somewhere in this city there are just a whole lot of people who could just do all those killings and flat walk *away*. Okay, stab, stab, and that's that. No worse than sticking a pig back on the farm. Anybody who has ever lived in the country knows *that*. And then it's a case of so much for that and what'll we have for supper tonight? *Crazy*? Look, you've got a man over there exposing himself in the *park* and nobody much cares. Standing there waving his *thing* and people see him and quickly look away. Lord. You walk out of the park and there's an old, old lady in raggy clothes carrying all those Lerner or Judy Bond shopping bags. And she's bent over and smelly and she's eating garbage out of one of those wire baskets on the sidewalk. Eating garbage and talking to herself. They're the ones who are crazy. There's a difference, Tony."

"I surrender," he said. "You got me."

"But there's something even worse than that," Nancy said.

He swung around to her. "What's worse?"

"Well, there *is*. Glory is right about the city. And you know what? The city will forget about all this. Seriously. These killings are *this* week. You know what will happen next week? Well, the Palestinian terrorists will seize the dumb Taft Hotel or someplace like that around the corner there. And they'll be holding eighty-hundred hostages, and they'll start shooting them and throwing them out all the windows. And there you go. You'll ask about the dead pimps and folks will look blank at you and say, 'Pimps? *What* pimps? Have you heard about the *hostages*?' See?"

"Are there any police jobs open in Oklahoma?" Olsen said.

"Okay. We'd better go," the sergeant said. "And if you all promise not to leap on me any more—no more shoptalk—I'll buy us all an after-dinner drink over at Jimmy Ryan's. I want to hear the cornet player. What I don't want to do is to talk business on my night off, all right?"

They came out the revolving doors and turned right, starting down toward Seventh Avenue. The sergeant stepped around to the street side, walking with his shoulder up close and rubbing; Nancy and Olsen fell into step behind.

The flurry of motion came all at once. She saw the man come

running around the corner from the poster store. He was moving fast toward them, dodging around people like a running back. He was wearing a zippered leather jacket and he was bareheaded. And then, suddenly, he was right there.

The shock of it half spun her around and it was like being hit hard in the shoulder when her purse swung out on its strap. Then the strap broke at the ring-buckle part and the loose end of it swung around free, trailing off behind the runner.

"*Lord*," she said. "Oh."

The sergeant whirled. "Wha . . ." he said.

"Purse," she said. "My *purse!*"

"Got him. That son of a bitch." Olsen took off in a crouching run, his raincoat flapping open. Then he stopped short on his heels, skidding. He swung his right hand around fast, flipping up the back of his suit coat, and came up with the gun. He held it out front, steadying it with his left hand. "Police officer!" he yelled. "Hold it right there or I shoot."

The man glanced back over his shoulder. Then he angled across the street toward the Roseland ballroom. He sidestepped around the front of a cab.

The sound of the gun going off was like a big iron door being slammed hard, and she could see Olsen's hands ride up from the force of it. Then he crouched a little bit more, legs apart, and fired again.

"My God," Nancy said, "you're going to kill him!"

Olsen half turned. "Son of a bitch," he said. "That son of a bitch. You wait right here." Then he wheeled around and started running toward Eighth Avenue, the gun still in his hand, pushing people out of the way with his other hand.

"My *purse*," Gloria said. "My . . ." She started a few steps after Olsen, then stopped. She turned back. "Never catch him."

The sergeant took her arm again. "Maybe Harv," he said. "He's pretty fast. Christ, aren't there any *cops* around here? Where in hell did that guy come from?"

She took a deep breath. Then she patted his hand where it was holding her by the forearm. "Oh, Tony. Lord, you *see?* You see what I mean now? It's just this dumb city, like I told you. It's full of crazy folks."

twenty-four

He looked up from the gray file folder and then rubbed at his eyes. "Just where the hell have you been?" he said.

Olsen hung his raincoat on the coatrack, walked over and sat down in the chair beside the desk. He stretched his legs out.

"Well," he said, "it took a little while to calm Gloria down after you left. She was still pretty goddamn hot about the purse. Stamping around up there. She can swear like a fucking cowboy, you know that? Anyway, after we got her calmed down and put to bed, Nancy and I mauled each other a little bit on the couch. You know."

"On my time?"

"You said this thing had to look right. You said, remember?"

"I know what I said. But . . ."

Olsen shrugged. "Well, then. But, look, I didn't really *do* it to her or anything; I was just doing what you said. She was too jumpy anyway. Afraid Gloria would get out of bed and come walking back into the front room. Besides, she kept bitching about me being married, like maybe it was my fault or something. So we just thrashed around a little, like at a drive-in movie. A little hand contact is all. And then I zipped up my pants and came back, soon as I figured it looked all right. But, anyway, the big thing is, what was in the purse?"

"Big thing, indeed. *Nothing* was in the purse. Naturally. I had half figured that much. Some keys. A Master Charge. Two dollars and some change. Subway tokens. Kleenex. A couple of Tampax, for Christ's sake. Nothing."

"Can't kill anybody with a Tampax."

"Will you knock it *off*, for Christ's sake? Jesus Christ, Harv. Come on. I can't think of a departmental rule we haven't broken so far and here you are, groping around on some couch with a fat broad. And there I am with one who sits there holding her mouth full of wine, looking at me coldly, like I'm some sort of an *exhibit* or something. This whole damn thing is screwed up."

"All right, I'm sorry. So what do we do now?"

He ran both hands through his hair, letting it spring up behind his fingers. "Well, what we do now is to put these two on hold for a while—maybe forever—and go back to the beginning again."

twenty-five

"YOU SURE DOAN LOOK like no *head*," he said. "What I mean is, if you was one once, you lookin' fine again now. Just fine."

Gloria held the heavy coffee mug in both hands, lifting it up and putting it back down on the Formica counter, bending her head to look under it where she was making a pattern of little wet rings with it, like Olympic circles. All the other pimps were talking loudly, all silky sounds, laughing in bursts. The place was all gray-blue with the smoke.

"The drying out took a long time," she said. "And it's lonely up there. You think they're treating you bad at first because it goes so slow. But I got it kicked and that's what counts. Except now I'm pretty stony, like I told you, and I've got to get it going again."

"Why me?" he said. "I mean, you a fly-lookin' chick. That blond hair and all. It's like honey, your hair. But you *sayin'* you been out of town, gettin' cured and all, and how am I supposed to *know*? Unnerstan' what I mean?"

She sighed again. "All right. Might as well tell you. You knew the Dancer?"

He slapped the counter with the palm of his hand. "Man, *knew* him? Harry, the dancin' man? Course I knew him; he came *in* here. Jivin' all the time, you know what I mean? Man, the Dancer was *killed* right over there. See out the window across the street? Right over there, baby. Man, he was talkin' on his car phone and some dude jumped out of a doorway in the rain and fair cut him to pieces. Took his *gizzard* out, unnerstan' what I mean?"

"I know," Gloria said. "They told me about it when I came back to town. And I read about it in the paper. And that's why I'm scared. I was—"

"You scared. We *all* scared. Everybody. I mean, snuffin' out them two cats at the hotel was somethin', but comin' right down to Eighth Avenue here, right here to this place, and takin' out the *Dancer*. Man. I mean, like we come out of here in *pairs* now, man, two at a time, with both of us just lookin' every which way. But *you* got nothin' to be scared about. I mean, the cutter ain't after no foxes. The cutter has only killed gentlemen of *leisure*, you dig it? Besides, you said you was what?"

She shrugged. "That's what I was trying to tell you. I just thought you knew. I was *with* the Dancer. Before I got sick."

He pulled back and looked at her, his eyebrows way up. "You was? Man, I didn't know that. Why din' you say so in the first place?"

"Don't talk so loud," she said. "Listen, I'm really scared. I mean, I came back from the hospital upstate and found the Dancer gone and now I haven't got any *man*, see? And what am I going to do? I got to have someone until I can get it all together again. I'm still weak."

He swung around again and leaned over closer. "I doan know." Then he raised his head and looked around. "Anybody else know about this?"

"Nobody. Look, if you don't want to—"

He took her arm. "No, wait a minute. Wait. I mean, maybe. I can dig it, unnerstan' what I mean? I can dig it. But how do I know that you ain't just assin' me around?"

"Well. Well, I don't know. You'll just have to—"

"You lookin' pretty peaked. For being so big and all. How do I know you can cut it? This ain't no personal *charity*, you know. You see these threads? Look here at this watch. See? Well, you come in with me, you get to be one of *my* girls, and you got to crank it out."

"I did it before," Gloria said. "The Dancer never complained."

"You was his bottom woman?"

"I won't lie to you. No. But I would have been."

He shook his head, looking into her eyes. And finally, he nodded. "Tell you what," he said. "I mean, I flat ain't takin' you no place to*night*. Uh *uh*. Man, I ain't no fool, you dig? But tell you what. Look here, it's early yet tonight, dig? And you can still get your buns out there yet."

"And?"

"And, you see that car over there? No, the white Caddie, second down from the corner. See it? Okay. That's *me*, baby. That's a *bad* car there, everythin' on it. Now then. You got tonight and *tomorrow*, dig it? And you know where Sixth Avenue is at?"

Gloria nodded, watching him. She began to smile.

"Well. Sixth Avenue and Fifty-four. Street goes east, you got it? Okay. Big hotels around there; all the out-of-town dudes with convention money. Dig it? You can work the Hilton; I got the guy there and they won't hassle you. But you don't *meet* me there. What you do is, you meet me on Fifty-four, like I said. Warwick Hotel on the corner, Dorset Hotel up toward the middle of the block. Fine, fine. I'll be up there, parked there, right-hand side, jus' up from the Dorset. Got it? And I'll be there—mmmm"—he looked at his watch, then punched the button so that the numbers flashed on in red—"I'll be there at one-fifteen ayem."

"Wish I had a watch like that," she said.

"They don't make them for foxes," he said. "But you do me right and you'll have one with real *stones* all around it, you dig? And a *fur* and things nice. Between now and then, you show me what you kin do and, I don't know, maybe we got us a thing. You and me. I could take care of you fine."

"One-fifteen," she said.

"I'll be there waitin'. I'll keep the engine runnin'."

She took a quick breath. "How much do you figure?"

He blinked a few times, thinking. "Ummm, three, four hundred. You any good at all. You shake your big white ass and you can do it easy. And if you was with the Dancer, you can do it laughin'."

"Three or four hundred," she said. She smiled at him. "I'll be there. I'll have it."

"See you," he said. "I got to split now. Places to go. People to see."

Gloria nodded. She reached over and patted him on the arm with her right hand. "Good night, honey-man," she said.

twenty-six

THEY STOOD ON THE SIDEWALK beside the Cadillac and watched the black panel truck pull away, headed east. The doctor took him by the arm, just above the elbow, and tugged gently. "Come on," he said. "Come on."

The sergeant looked at him, blinking. "You know, this thing absolutely beats the shit out of me," he said. "Just about every time I think I can get some kind of a handle on it, *this* happens. I can't figure out what the hell is going on around here."

The doctor pulled again, harder. "Come on. I'm going to take you over across the street here and we'll get some coffee. And I'm going to give you some pills I want you to take. Are you listening to me, Tony?"

"Right out on the goddamned street," the sergeant said. "The street here. Midtown. People walking up and down. And the horn honking. How long was the horn honking like that before somebody thought to look inside the car? Chrissakes, the guy might as well have hired a hall. So somebody finally—*finally*—looks into the car. And what do they find?"

The doctor nodded at him again, looking him closely in the eyes. "Same thing. I know. You know. The old slasher strikes again. You saw it. Did everything but put the guy's balls in the glove compartment. Listen, you really look lousy, I'll say that for you. Don't you ever sleep?"

"I was asleep. Well, no. I was almost asleep. What I was doing was lying there, looking up at the ceiling, trying to figure things out. My life. This case. You do that a lot when you live in one room. You lie half awake, just on the edge."

"That's no good," the doctor said. "I mean, medically it's no good. Just being half asleep is about as good for you as having half a hard on."

"Mmmm, maybe. But the thing is, during the day you chase a bunch of thoughts around inside your head, squeezing hard to get at them. And they keep eluding you, right? But in that half-awake stage, when your brain unclenches, they finally just sort of seep back in."

"If you say so. You're getting out of my field. You guys are keeping me too busy around here with these goddamn home-made pimp vasectomies, for Christ's sake. Now, are you coming to get that coffee, or do I have to—"

"That's what I mean. Pimps. Why pimps?"

"Huh? How would I know?"

The sergeant shrugged. "Well, that's what I mean. I just about had it doped out when the phone rang with this thing. And then, the first time I looked inside that Caddie, I thought I had it figured out again. It was something somebody said to me. It was at dinner. I was trying to be clever at the time and I was fucking it up. But anyway, the comment was that pimps need killing pretty bad because they hurt people pretty bad."

"So?"

"So do pimps go around hurting each other? Uh uh. The idea is, they hurt *women*. Jesus, I'm really tired, you know that? Anyway, between that and the Caddie here, that's about it."

"You're talking in circles, DeMario. What about the Caddie here?"

"It's a hunch, and I never play hunches. Well, I've played a couple recently and got burned on both of them. So never again. But it keeps coming back to me at odd times."

The doctor patted at his raincoat pockets. "This is an odd enough time. Listen, have you got a cigarette?"

The sergeant lit it for him. "Just answer me one thing."

"I'm yours."

"You ever see two pimps sitting together in the same car?"

"I've never looked."

"Well, I have. And they don't, usually. Their car is their own private little kingdom. It's theirs, their territory."

"The kingdom usually belongs to Household Finance."

"Doesn't matter. What counts is, it's possible that the someone who was inside this Caddie here was not a pimp. Probably not, in fact. Which shoots my theory about the pimp war, in a way. But if it wasn't a pimp, then who would it be?"

"Customer?"

"Maybe."

"Hooker?"

The sergeant nodded at him. "Maybe. But not another pimp. And once I get that through my head, it narrows it down a whole lot."

"Oh, sure. You eliminate pimps and that narrows it down to just men and women."

"And who do pimps hurt the most?"

"What am I, your goddamn straight man? Okay, Mr. Bones, they hurt women the most."

"Uh huh." The sergeant walked back over to the Caddie and leaned against the back fender and crossed his legs. "Uh *huh*." He looked around, both ways on the street, up at the windows on the buildings. He jammed his hands deeper into his raincoat pockets. "Okay, then, listen. What about all those trick pills you were going to give me to make me sleep?"

twenty-seven

SHE CAME HOME EARLY to get the apartment straightened up for Barry—but mostly to turn on the television and watch for anything about the pimp on the six o'clock news.

She poured some wine into the big-bowled glass and carried it into the front room, pausing to kick off her shoes, then switched on the set and sat down on the floor. She raised up straight to undo the snap on her jeans where it was pinching her stomach, then slumped forward, her forearms resting on her knees.

This time she was calm, breathing easily, and she had her face set just right; cold and stand-away. There was no need to look obliquely at the little screen anymore, or to go through the ritual of pushing off anything bad by wishing it away. Nothing could happen now; the TV reporter looking directly into the camera would not be looking directly into her eyes—and if he was, it wouldn't make any difference now anyway. She could look directly back at him, look back at anybody now. The job was done and the city was a little better. That's it. That's all, no more.

The face on the screen turned out to be the woman TV reporter, the one who was so terrible that the only possible reason they let her get on the air was that she was the token house black. She did all the sister-donates-kidney-to-dying-brother reports. Or else she always seemed to be interviewing somebody who was lying in a hospital bed with tubes sticking up their noses. The people mostly just laid there, squinting into the hand-held camera lights, and just nodded at the dumb questions, yes nods and no nods, embarrassed to be on television after surviving the plane crash at La Guardia.

Now the reporter was standing beside the white Caddie on 54th Street, inside the police roped-off area, talking into a microphone with the spongy black ball on top of it. She was telling about how a man had been killed and all cut up inside this car.

Gloria nodded, watching. She sipped at the wine. Uh huh. Right so far, little old black lady.

The blowing horn had done it. A cabdriver who had just dropped someone off at the Dorset Hotel had driven by the Cadillac and had stopped to yell at the horn blower to knock it off. He had looked in and had seen all the blood on the man and blood on the steering wheel and the dashboard, and he had jumped out of his cab and had gone around to take a closer look.

"I mean to tell ya it was something awful," the cabby was saying now, talking to the black lady reporter. "Sheesh. I mean, like there was blood on . . ."

While he was talking, the picture changed and the television camera looked into the car. But the lighting was not strong enough and the stains didn't really look like much. Especially in black and white.

Then there was another shot, taped just outside the 17th Precinct on 51st Street, where the woman reporter tried to talk to Tony DeMario, who was being jostled by a bunch of reporters in front of the doorway. He looked at the microphone stuck up under his nose like it was a snake's head or something and just shook his head no.

"Any new leads on this latest . . ." the black lady was saying, but Tony just shouldered her aside and went in through the door.

"No new leads," Gloria said to the screen. "No old leads, no new leads, you dumb-ass black lady."

Behind her head, she could hear all the locks clicking, and she swung around and nodded at Nancy coming in.

"Okay. Before I say anything," Nancy said, "you in a bad mood again?"

Gloria leaned over and switched off the set. "No, *good* mood. Good. Come on. Have I been all that terrible?"

"Oh, no. Lord, no, you've just been fine. It's just like living with Elizabeth *Taylor* or somebody like that. Like some cat-lady or something. In and out at night until all hours—and then grouchy in between. Moody. Other than a bunch of little things like that, you've been swell."

"All right, I'm sorry. Really. I know. Just been going through one of my things, I guess. I get so . . . well. But it's all over now and I promise to be better. Okay?" She uncrossed her legs and got up to her knees and then closed the waist snap again. "Anyway, look, I'm going to pick everything up around here. I'll straighten up the kitchen, too."

"Don't lose your head."

"No, I'll do it. Listen, Barry's coming by for a drink. All right?"

Nancy crossed her arms in front and took hold of the sides of her sweater. She pulled it up over her head, then paused and looked out through the neck opening. "Coming by when?"

"I don't know. Pretty soon, I guess. Why?"

Nancy pulled the sweater the rest of the way off and then shook her arms out of the sleeves. She threw it down on the couch. "Well, for one thing, guess who called me at work today? No, don't guess; it was Harvey Olsen. And guess what I told him?"

"You told him to come on by for a drink," Gloria said.

"Uh huh. I did."

"Well, *swell*. I mean, you just sort of said to come on up for a drink."

"Yes. I don't know, I just said it. I just"—Nancy looked down at her breasts and then she shrugged—"said it."

"Well, for God's *sake*, Nancy. Harvey Olsen is *married*. I mean, you know that."

Nancy looked up. "I know, I know. But he called. And he . . . well, I don't know. I mean, he said something about a pixie haircut and all that kind of stuff and . . . Oh, shit, Gloria. I don't know."

"Well, that's flat *dumb*."

Nancy walked over and sat down on the couch. She leaned forward and straightened the magazines on the coffee table, carefully lining up the edges. "Well, I suppose Barry *Harkner* isn't married? He's even worse than that. He's married and he's *Jewish*. At least Harvey Olsen is a *Baptist*. Good Lord. And Barry Harkner is *fat*, too."

"Oh, for Christ's *sake*, Nancy. I know all that. Look, you don't even half begin to understand the problems I have. I know Barry is Jewish. What the hell. Everybody in *town* is Jewish. I don't give the faintest—"

"Your mother would have kittens."

"Well, *screw* my mother. What I mean is, I'm not mooning over Barry like some dumb little old high-school cheerleader. I'm not sitting out here giving him *hand* jobs on that goddamn couch like you did Harvey Olsen. I heard you out here; I wasn't asleep that night."

"Well, what if I *did?* What of it? You must be giving Barry something-jobs," Nancy said. "Don't give me that bullshit."

"Well, I'm *not.* Don't look at me like that. I'm not. You don't understand, like I said. I just happen to *need* Barry right now; I need him to help get my head straight. Hell, yes. Sure, we'll make it if I can ever bring myself to do it. But that's something else. Listen, I'll fuck him right there on the couch, all over this bullshit dumb apartment, if I ever can. What I mean is, I'm not falling in love. Mooning around. You know, touching him on the arm across the table and all that Mia Farrow horseshit. Jesus Christ, Nancy."

"Well, don't you dare shout at me. It doesn't make Barry any less married, I don't give a goddamn what you say. Jesus CHRIST, Gloria."

"Okay, okay. So what becomes of you and Harvey? Answer me that, dummy. What? Listen, I don't want Barry for good. Not for *keeps.* His sad old little-titted wife can have him back any time she wants. When I'm *through.* That's when. He can go back to his dumb Long Island, catch his dumb damn trains at night, I don't care. But I come first."

"He's still fat."

"Not that fat, he isn't."

Nancy put both hands down on the table and messed the magazines all around again. "Well, that's *fine.* Just fine. Lord, at least I'm not *using* Harvey Olsen like that. Not me. Boy, you got some kind of *mean* streak in you, Gloria."

"It isn't either mean. My ass it's mean. It's right, that's what it is. It's what's right for me. I'm just being *honest,* like everybody else should be in this crazy town, and you only think it's being mean. If something is wrong, you just flat fix it. Somebody has to. Nobody else looks out for anybody else around here. And—"

"You were even mean when you were a kid. Those Pulver boys. They—"

"Uh huh. There you go: the Pulver boys. You always bring them up again. Okay. They would tie up some old dog down at the railroad tracks, down there by the monument works, remember? And they would stand off and peg rocks at it and stone it to death. Well, who looked after the poor old *dog?* I'll tell you who. *Me.* Those buggers."

"You stole your daddy's pool cue and—"

"Bet your cheerleading ass I did. And the one I missed—uh—Jody. I went up to their front porch that night and whistled for him to come out. And when he came out on the porch, I like to bust his fucking *head* open. Christ, he couldn't even *see* straight enough after that to hit anything with a rock. Well, you see, somebody had to do it; it just turned out to be me. Hadn't been me, it would have been somebody else. Goddamn, you're dumb. That's not *mean.* That's getting things *done.* Anyway, where in the hell was I? Oh. No, I'm not being mean to Barry. In fact, I really half love him, that old . . . well. What it is, I happen to *need* him right now. And if I can work it out just right, okay. If I can do it, then everything will be gentle again. That's all."

"Listen," Nancy said. "Listen to me, will you? Wait a minute. Why are we fighting? I mean, why are you yelling at me? Your face is all splotchy, for God's sake. We got to stop it. What it is, is that we're both in the same dumb situation here, and here we we are *yelling* at each other. Come on. I'll stop it if you will. And anyway, what troubles? What do you mean, bring yourself to do it? You never told me."

"Well, I . . ." She stopped and took a deep breath. "Let me get everything calmed down here for a second. Listen, Nance, I'm sorry. Okay? Just let me breathe a second."

"Sit down," Nancy said. "Look, I'll get you some more wine."

Gloria sank to the floor and crossed her legs. She put her elbows up on the coffee table. "Thanks. Get some for you, too."

Nancy came back in with the wine. "Here. Come on. I'm sorry, too. We'll never do it again, all right? But you didn't ever tell me."

"What's there to tell? I just . . . Look, will you go in and put something on, for God's sake? You're going to catch pneumonia of the boobs or something, going around like that."

Nancy crossed her arms in front. "Oh, and another thing. I heard what you said about little tits. Well, hell. I mean, everybody can't be big like you. You know."

"I know. I'm sorry I said it."

"And Mia Farrow."

"Oh, fuck Mia Farrow," Gloria said. "I'm sorry I said that, too. I don't know what got into me."

"But tell me about the other thing."

"Well, it's just that I can't seem to *do* it. And Barry is big and he's gentle and he seems to be just right. But we haven't . . . so far, we haven't. It's funny. There are times when I'm all alone and I get this really great sort of—uh—horny surge, and if I could just conjure him up at exactly that moment, well, we could do it. But when he's *here,* and when we get right to that point, well, I sort of freeze up. I want to. But I can't."

"How does Barry feel about it?"

"Oh, patient. You know, guilty, patient. A lot of things. I never ask him. I just worry about me."

Nancy nodded. "But maybe it's physical. You know. Maybe if a gynecologist—"

"No, no. My plumbing's all right. Everything's there. The magic button, all of it. You know."

"Okay. But if that's the case, what you should do is talk to someone. Someone pro*fess*ional, I mean. No, don't look at me like that. I'm serious. Listen, I did it. When I first came to town, I mean. I never told you. But it helped. No, better than that. It fixed me up. Just going to an analyst, the idea, the routine of going, someone to talk to. See, sometimes folks need to. You, me, the girls we know at the office. We all talk about it. Well, not everything, not all the details. That's between you and the analyst. But you find out that other people are seeing them too and it makes you feel better, see? It forms a kind of a, well, a bond, like. Maybe it's being single and working here in New York. Especially in a place like a newsmagazine, where there are a lot of single girls and a lot of married men and all the sexual pressures. You work on a story with a guy—working late and under deadlines—and you get close to him, like you're sharing a secret. And you find yourself wondering what his cock looks like. The pressure is all on the researchers. Big, wonderful man has written or edited a story, something you can't do, and pretty soon big, wonderful man is kissing you on the neck and he's going rubbie-rubbie right here, up and down, and you *like* it. It's tough. Researcher-fucking is like a writer's reward or something. I don't know."

"You never told me," Gloria said. "Never."

"I know. But you always seemed to have everything so all worked out. So perfect. I thought maybe you wouldn't understand. You're always so cool. Always know what to do."

"I wear it like a mask."

"Huh. You'd never know. Ever."

"What was your thing?" Gloria said. "I mean, if you want to tell me."

Nancy shrugged. "I went the other way when I came to town. About men, I mean. It wasn't a case of not being able to do it. I got here from Greer and I got this apartment and all and, Christ, all I wanted to do was to jump *up* on guys. You know. I even went to a gynecologist then. I thought maybe I had an overactive buzzer or something. But then I found Dr. Goldener. Janie —you know, from the office—she had been seeing her. And she—"

"Her?"

"Sure, her. She's a woman. You don't think I'd tell a man about all that stuff? Listen, Gloria-Ann, maybe you ought to try it. It can't hurt; you know, about what you just told me. About your—uh—block."

"No, I don't need it. But if it fixed you up so good, well, what about Harvey Olsen? Don't jump now, I'm not going to yell at you anymore."

Nancy shook her head. "I know, I know. But, see, Harvey is the first guy in . . . Well, I haven't been doing too much, you know that. I don't seem to have men falling all over me so much anymore. Far from it. At work, even. But then Harvey called me up. It was just like that, and we talked and finally I said to come over for a drink. And then I thought about it and I realized that, while he had been talking to me, about the only picture that came into my mind was him shooting that *gun*. Oh, God, I could have thrown him down right then, on the street there. And then I thought about, you know, well, about our being here on the couch and him wearing that gun. I mean, wearing it while we're *doing* it. Anyway, look, I know he's married. But, see, he's thinking about leaving his wife. They don't get along. He told me that night he was here. So maybe it'll all work—"

"I think they all say that," Gloria said. "It's part of the thing. Barry told me."

"Well, what does Barry say?"

"Oh, he gets along with his wife just fine. Well, he did. For all

I know, he's sleeping at the office half the time now. But he'll go back to her. When I'm through."

Nancy looked up. "Hey, wait a sec. What time is it?"

"Oh, shit. Listen, they could be here any minute."

"I'll go change," Nancy said. She stood up. "What the hell will I put on?"

"Wear what you've got. Harvey would love to see you topless."

"No, really."

"He's going to get down to those little rascals sooner or later tonight."

"Who said? Well, not right away, he's not. And if he doesn't take me out to dinner, he's not going to get down to them at all. I don't give a damn how little they are."

"Well, go put something on. Hurry it up."

"Look, can you get up some stuff while I'm changing? I don't know. Maybe some wine and whatever. Cheese and crackers or something."

"Okay. Go on."

Nancy turned at the door. "Aren't you going to change?"

"What for? For Barry? No, I'll just unbutton another button and sprinkle some of your stuff right here. He always manages to get his big old nose down in there anyway; he'll love it."

"Okay. I'll hurry."

Gloria went into the kitchen and got out the cheese board and the wire slicer. She started to cut the cheese, humming, leaning her stomach against the counter. She took a handful of the slices and arranged them on the tray, then paused, holding her hand in the air. She picked one up again and looked closely at the edge of it. She put it back down and reached over and got her wineglass and sipped some more of the wine, looking at the slices on the tray. Then she straightened briefly and reached into her right front pocket and lifted out the razor. She got it balanced just right in the palm of her hand and then rolled her hand over to open the blade. She held down the block of Cheddar with her left hand and began cutting with her right, watching the orange slices roll away smoothly, each one curling out slightly when the convex side of the blade came down. She had begun to hum again, slicing, when the doorbell rang.

"I'll get it," she said.

She tore off a section of paper towel and wiped the blade

clean, holding it up to the light and looking closely at it. Then she rolled it closed and put it back into her pocket on the way to the door.

She looked through the peephole and then undid all the locks.

"Hey," Olsen said.

"Hey, yourself."

"Say something to me in Oklahoma."

"Oh, Christ, come on in, Harvey. Don't stand there."

He came in and stood to one side while she locked the door again. "No, seriously, are you feeling any better now? Look, we've had the purse-snatching detail out all—"

"Oh, forget it," Gloria said. "It's just about like you protecting us from the burglars. Some protection."

"I'm really sorry about it, Gloria."

"Forget it."

"No, really. I—"

"Harvey."

He shrugged. "All right, all right. Listen, where's—"

"She'll be out in a minute."

"Okay. Uh . . . well. Can I sit down?" He walked into the front room and sat on the couch. "Oh. Tony says to say hello."

"Tony who?"

He looked up. "Gloria, let me up, will you? I *said* I was sorry about the purse. Anyway, it sure wasn't Tony's fault. I think he wants to call you, but I guess he's bashful."

"I didn't get that impression."

"Well, he's been busy, for one thing."

"Haven't we all."

Nancy came to the door and paused, looking at them. "Hello out there."

Olsen stood up. "Hi, pixie girl."

Nancy glanced quickly at Gloria. "Uh . . . yes, Harvey. Uh, well . . ."

He looked at Gloria. "What are you grinning at?"

She shrugged. "Nothing. Nothing at all. Listen, we're all having red wine. Mostly because red wine is all we have to offer. And some cheese and crackers, all right?"

He nodded. "That'll be fine. I'm off duty. I mean, Tony gave me the night off."

"He must not be all that busy, then."

"Well, he isn't, really. Just the usual routine stuff. In fact, it's pretty dull down there."

She went into the kitchen and put the wineglasses on the tray. Then she lifted the half gallon of Gallo Hearty Burgundy and poured it. She was carrying in the tray when the doorbell rang.

"Go ahead, I'll get it," Nancy said. She looked through the peephole and unlocked everything and swung the door open. "Hello, Barry."

He looked in. "I didn't know you had company," he said. He put his hands into his pants pockets. His toes were pointed out.

"Well, come on in."

He walked in and stood, looking at Harvey.

"This is Harvey Olsen," Gloria said. "Harvey, this is Barry Harkner. Harvey. Barry."

Barry nodded. "Hello."

"Hi, Barry. What was it? Harknuh?"

"Hark*ner*. Harkner."

"Got it. Well, then. Like some red wine?"

"I'd love some," Barry said.

"Barry, for heaven's sake, come in and sit down," Gloria said. "Come on, now."

They sat side by side on the couch. Barry leaned forward and put both hands around the bowl of the wineglass. He glanced over at Olsen. "Well."

Olsen nodded. "Well. Uh . . . what line of business are you in, Harkner?"

"I write."

"That's it?"

"Mmmm hmmm. *Time* magazine."

"Oh? I read it. All the time. What—uh—what stuff do you write in there?"

"Oh, this and that. A lot of things."

"Uh huh. You live here in town?"

Barry swallowed and put the wineglass down. "No. Out on the Island."

"Oh. You commute home every night, I guess?"

"Except those nights that I stay in town, yes."

Gloria brought the bottle in and poured some more wine. "Knock it off, Harvey," she said. "Tell us where you commute to every night."

He blinked up at her. "Well, I was just making conversation."

"Sure you were."

"Listen," Nancy said. "Listen, Harvey, are you going to take me out to dinner or not?"

He nodded. "I'm definitely going to take you out to dinner."

"And what do you do, Olsen?" Barry said.

"Me? I'm a detective."

"Oh. Private?"

"No. Public."

"What do you detect?"

"About what?"

"No. I mean, what is your forte?"

Harvey blinked. "Well, I'm in homicide. Zone Three."

"Listen," Nancy said, "come on, you guys. Uh, where are you going to take me to dinner?"

"I don't know. Gallagher's? House of Chan?"

"No," Gloria said. "We're going to the House of Chan."

"We are?" Barry said.

"We are."

Olsen put his wineglass down and stood. "Well, I guess we had better get going. What do you say, pixie?"

"Nancy," she said. "The name is Nancy." She looked over at Gloria. And she shrugged.

"No, wait!" Gloria said. "Holy smokes. I forgot the cheese and crackers. You can't go yet. Wait a minute, everybody. Now, you-all have just one more glass of wine here. Just a second."

She went into the kitchen and looked down at the cheese tray, at the curled slices of Cheddar that she had cut with the razor. Then she picked up the tray and carried it back into the front room. She bent over in front of each one.

"Everybody take a piece of cheese," she said. "No. Not that one. Everybody has to take one of the curly ones."

Then she stood up and watched them, each of them holding a piece of the cheese. And each one raised it slowly and ate it while she smiled down at them.

"*Take, eat: this is my body, which is broken for you. This is a new testament in my blood.*"

It was just like a Holy Sacrament.

twenty-eight

SHE WAS PROMOTED to researcher the next morning and the first thing she did was call Maintenance and order one of the name tags. It would slide into the slot just outside the glass door of her new office, clean white letters stamped into the black fiberboard: GLORIA-ANN COOPER. And she went right around to the other corridor to tell Barry.

He was sitting the way he sometimes did when he was writing something complicated and couldn't think of what to write, perched on the edge of his swivel chair, legs apart, hands dangling down between his knees. He was leaning far forward, his forehead resting against his typewriter just above where it said Royal.

The first time Gloria had seen him sitting this way, it had surprised her. But when he had explained, it wasn't all as dumb as it looked.

"Very simple, my dear," he had said. "Some writers lean back in their chairs and put their feet on the desk, scowling, perhaps even showing a touch of froth at the mouth. Some others look out the windows with unseeing eyes. Or they lock their hands behind their heads and look up at the ceiling panels. Well, I choose to rest my forehead against this typewriter here. For one thing, it's cooling. For another, since I pour all my thoughts into this infernal machine every day, I keep half hoping that maybe the damn thing will pour some thoughts back into my head. You see?"

He was sitting that way now, motionless, his eyes almost closed. Finally she cleared her throat.

He turned his head to look at the doorway, not lifting his forehead from the typewriter housing. "Hello, there," he said. "You coughed?"

"I'm a researcher now," Gloria said. "Me. Just now."

He got up heavily and tugged at the front of his shirt where it was twisted under his belt. Then he came around the desk and kissed her on the left cheek first, then the right one. "Wonderful. Congratulations and all that. The career of Glory Cooper moves inexorably ahead, right? More money, I guess?"

"A lot more. I mean, it will be. I'm going out at lunch and buy a bunch of stuff."

"Fine, fine."

"And then, I'm—" She stopped and looked at him. "What's the matter?"

"Me?" He put his hands in his pockets. "Nothing, nothing. You were saying that you were going out to buy some things."

"Well, I—"

"Well, I said fine."

"But—"

"Perhaps some more sexy underwear. By all means, more underwear. I believe that I have . . . well, no. As far as I know, I think I have seen everything in your current collection."

"Underwear?"

"Isn't that the right word? Underpants. Panties." He shrugged. "Those little bikini things with all the flowers. Some have lace around the waistband."

"And so?"

"And so nothing. It was merely a comment."

"It wasn't either," she said. "Come on, Bear. What—"

"I particularly like the ones with all the little blue flowers against the green background. With that ever-so-tiny little name printed in among them in script. If you look closely, very closely, it says 'Emilio' over and over again. As you will recall, that was last night's pair."

She breathed in deeply. "All right," she said. "Stop it. Come on. If you're going to talk about last night, I don't care to hear any more. I told you I was sorry. I *said*, remember?"

He went back around the desk, swung the chair and sat down.

He stared at the typewriter for a few minutes, then looked back at her. "You said. You did, indeed. Right."

"Well, I was. I *am* sorry, I mean."

"I know the feeling well," he said.

"But you told me it was all right. You know, you—"

He nodded. "I know. That was then. But this is . . . well. This is probably ruining my entire reproductive system, among other things. We seem to start so well. It's those closing moments, I mean, those nonclosing moments, that are doing me in. What was it that the writer said? Something about the penultimate caress."

"Bear."

He waved at the typewriter, then slapped it with his hand. "And now. Now I'm past deadline, and I can't write. And I'm sleepy; I'm so *tired*. I slept on the couch here last night, and when I woke up this morning, I could smell your body on the palms of my hands. And I called home and my wife wouldn't let me say good morning to my little girl. I always say good morning to her if I'm . . . uhhh. She's only *little* and she likes to talk on the telephone. But my wife—"

"Barry."

"I don't know. I seem to be . . . Well, I *don't* seem to be thinking properly here. It's not like me. Not like me at all."

"Barry, I . . . no. We'll call it off. You can go home. Just go back."

He shook his head. "Back? It's too late. I'm sitting here more or less drenched in guilt and—mmmm—God knows what else. Remorse? All right, remorse. And still I know that it's too late. Look, I'm too old to suffer from whatever this is; this happens to young men. Unrequited love. Too old. But I'm suffering nonetheless. It's more than just the sex. Huh. *That's* the wrong thing to say. The lack of sex. It's more than that. You came walking in here a few weeks ago from God knows where, all big and alive, and you gave off a . . . something. A vitality. And I looked at you and I knew you were in there, somewhere. And I . . ."

She looked at him for a long moment. "Bear," she said, "I'm going to go."

". . . and I need . . ."

"So long, Bear."

Nancy and Janie had the champagne ready when she got back to her new office. There were two bottles of Taylor New York

State sitting on the gray desk, and one of the other girls had brought around the plastic take-out glasses with the pop-off stems.

She stood in the doorway for a moment, biting at her lower lip and breathing deeply, until they looked up and saw her.

"My name tag come up yet?" she said.

"Up? God's sake, it was about six minutes ago you ordered it. Give them a little time. Lord, I always have trouble with these plastic corks. Hold on. Easy now, here it comes. There." Nancy poured the champagne into the little glasses and they all picked one up. "Okay, everybody got some? Well, here's to the new researcher. Welcome to the Land of the Living Dead."

Gloria held it in her mouth and let the bubbles fizz out on the roof of her mouth. Then she swallowed. She looked around at the gray swivel chair with its dirty tweedish sort of seat and gray Naugahyde armrests, the brown carpet, and the whitish walls with all the tack punctures in them. She reached over and slid the glass door back and forth a few times.

"I'll fix this place up nice," she said. "Put a lot of good stuff on the walls."

"More bubbles?" Nancy said.

"Mmmm hmmm, fill it up. Easy, don't get any on my desk. See over there? I'll put a big bullfight poster right there. You know. Manolete or whoever."

"Except I wish they had one where the bull wins," Janie said. "Sticks that old horn right up the guy's ass. But I've got to admit, he looks good in those spangled pants."

They toasted again.

"I'm going out at lunch and spend money," Gloria said. "Anybody want to come along?"

Nancy shrugged. "If you buy about one more blouse, there won't be any room left in the apartment. And underpants. God, nothing but pants hanging over the shower rod."

"All through buying fancy pants," Gloria said. "That's all over and done. In fact, I'll never have to buy any again. Next pair I get are just going to be plain cotton drawers. Ones made out of Serta Perfect mattress ticking. Flour sacks. I don't know. Mr. Emilio Pucci can stick it in his ear. Now, then. If you'll all kindly leave me alone in my new office, I'm going to sit down here and slide my door closed and look around. All right?"

When they had gone, she sat down in the chair and put her

forearms on the armrests. She swiveled it around a few times. Then she pushed back against the backrest and put her feet up on the top of the desk.

She could feel the curved line of the razor in her right front pocket, fitted tight into the crease between her thigh and where her pubic hair bunched up.

This was a whole new life beginning; maybe she could throw the thing away now. Dump it down the incinerator chute and let them take it off to the dump and burn it with the others. Maybe —maybe not. She'd have to think . . .

She jumped a bit when the telephone rang. Then she swung her feet down and yanked open the top desk drawer and got out a pencil. She pulled the yellow lined note pad over close and picked up the phone.

"Gloria-Ann Cooper's line," she said.

The voice was a lot smokier than she remembered. "Good morning," he said. "Detective Sergeant DeMario. May I speak to Miss Cooper, please?"

Old wolfy teeth. She threw down the pencil. "This is her. Uh, she."

"I thought so," he said. "That accent. Glory, I've got your purse over here. It was picked up late last night. Nothing in it, but I've got it."

"Swell. Nothing in it."

"Well, that's to be expected. They haven't got the thief yet, the report says. But they will. Would you like to have me send—"

"No," she said. "You can keep it."

"All right. Strap seems to be broken here anyway. I'm really sorry, like I said. But—"

"I know. Just one of those things that happen here in New York, right? Don't worry about it."

"Okay. And one more thing."

Uh huh. Naturally. One more thing. And guess what that's going to be. "Hmmm?" she said.

"Would you like to have dinner tonight?"

"What for?"

"Well, let's see, now. For one thing, we'll both be hungry sometime this evening, right? But, no. The main reason is that I'd just like to see you again."

She glanced down at her breasts. "Uh huh. Well, it was nice of you to ask, but I'm afraid—"

"Look, I'll try to take better care of you. This time I'll carry your purse, okay?"

"No. You see, I—"

The motion made her look up. Barry was standing in the doorway, looking in at her. His tie was pulled around so that half the knot was up under one point of his collar. His eyes were red. She nodded at him and then turned away.

"I know a place," Tony said. "Only police officers eat there. Not a purse snatcher within miles."

She nodded. "Well, I—"

"Come on. I need to look at you."

She pushed herself back into her chair a little more. For some reason, she could feel the front seam of her jeans where it went down and around. She thought about the stuff all drying over the shower rod back at the apartment. And some on the towel rack. Then she took a quick breath. "Okay," she said. "Fine. Just come on by after work and pick me up. Maybe seven-thirty, something like that. It'll give me time to get home and change clothes."

twenty-nine

THE FIRST TIME at the psychiatrist, Gloria just sat there, toes curled down inside her shoes, looking at her hands in her lap. She talked in rambling sentences, all the unimportant stuff, for almost an hour. That was seventy dollars' worth.

And now she was sitting in the padded beige leather chair again, staring at the tropical plant just over the doctor's left shoulder, not blinking, holding her mouth just exactly right.

"Any time now," the doctor said.

"I know," Gloria said. "I'm just thinking about where to start."

She had finally decided to go ahead and do this only because Nancy and Janie had sounded so damned convincing. And after the thing with Tony—which she hadn't told Nancy about.

Everybody goes; everybody needs some reassurance and counseling of some sort, Janie kept saying. It wasn't really so much to cure anything. It was if you were single and living in New York, say. It was to help keep the city from driving you crazy. And it could. It was dehumanizing, Janie had said. All right, then.

"A shrink isn't guaranteed to pick you right up and turn you around," Nancy had said. "I mean, you don't get a whole new life every time. A shrink just pounds out a few of the dents in your armor. But that's just about all anybody really needs, anyway; it's just that you can't do it all by yourself."

The more they had gone on about it, the more sense it had made. This certain analyst had helped her find her real sexual identity, Janie had said. Not that she figured Gloria had any such problem. Gloria's problem was her ups and downs. "You're either feeling super or you're all pissed off about something and won't even talk to any of us. Well, listen to old Janie. Dr. Goldener can help."

Dr. Goldener was Dr. Laura Goldener, with a long string of initials after her name on the door; a thick, solid woman who wore a lot of beads and smoked a lot and had mussy hair like reddish steel wool. She did not insist that anybody lie down on the couch. Gloria had looked at it sort of fearfully when she had first come into the room.

"Sit down, lie down on the floor, hang by your heels. I don't give a damn," Dr. Goldener had said. "The role of the analyst's couch is vastly overrated in counseling. And so is the image of the psychiatrist sitting behind the desk chewing thoughtfully on one leg of a pair of eyeglasses while listening to you talk. It's the crap you see on television, not here. And you might as well know right now that I don't intend to talk to you in psychiatric mumbo jumbo. I will most certainly not tell you that you suffer from a sexual dysfunction when what I really mean is that you can't get it off. All right? Those are my rules. You be totally honest with me and I'll be honest right back at you in words that you can understand. Now, the first hour will probably be shot all to hell because you'll spend all the time fencing with me, telling me things that I don't really need to hear. But that's the way it always goes. After that, if you're convinced that I can help, we can get down to work."

All right, then. She had it figured out now. She knew exactly what things she was, and what things she was not, going to tell the doctor. Not about the razor, no. For one thing, that was certainly not a problem. It was safe right here in the pocket of her jeans, and when she crossed her right leg over, she could feel the warm bend of it in tight against the upper inside of her thigh. Nothing to talk to a doctor about there. No, what she would talk about was the problem. She shifted her eyes from the potted plant and looked directly at the doctor.

"Well, what if I—uh—if maybe I do suffer from a sexual—uh— what you said last week. Dysfunction."

Dr. Goldener nodded. "Well, now, that's a start. I thought perhaps we were going to spend another entire session in which you did nothing but tell me your name, rank and serial number. All right. There are degrees of this sort of trouble. Do you mean that you don't have satisfactory orgasms? Or orgasms at all? Or what?"

"I don't . . . I can't. Well, hell. I don't even get to the dumb orgasm part. It's before *that*, even."

"Okay. Tell me a little bit more."

"Well," Gloria said. "Well, okay, then. I get passionate, just like everybody does. And I really like all the hugging and the kissing and the feeling *around* that, you know, that leads up to it. I—uh—I'm not sure I know how to put this. But there are times when I get a sudden quick surge of love and I feel like I could just sort of . . . well, you know, sort of grab somebody and stuff him right up IN there. It's a tender feeling, really; like wrapping my arms and legs all around him and hunching my back over and hiding him from sight. Protecting him, even. Okay. But then there's the bad part. It always starts when . . . well, it's like when he rolls over to get up on top of me and suddenly I feel all unprotected and helpless. That's it. I mean, I'm there on my back and my legs are all open, my *God*, and I'm kind of pinned down by it all. And then suddenly I feel like maybe someone is going to get *to* me. Well, *nobody* gets to me; I won't let them, see? And then I get sort of sick. Angry-sick, really, and my stomach tightens all up and I feel barfy. And then I can't do it." She paused, blinking, breathing hard. "And that's it."

"Fine, fine. Keep going."

Gloria scowled at her. "I told you, I just *told* you. You're the one who's supposed to fix it."

Dr. Goldener nodded. "And I'll *try*, Gloria. Now just settle down. I just need to know more. That's all. Here, have a cigarette." She leaned across the desk and lit it. "Now then, have you ever managed to go through with it? All the way through it?"

"No. Well, yes. When I was a little girl. It was done to me."

"I'll be direct. Was it your father?"

"No, *no*. I've read all about that junk. No."

"Did you do it often as a kid?"

"I *said* no."

"All right. And later. After you were grown up?"

"Ummm, once. When I first came to town. No, it was more than once, I guess. I don't know."

"We'll get back to that. The point is: never to climax?"

"Oh, for God's *sake*."

"Easy, Gloria. We're perking right along here now. Tell me, have you *ever* climaxed? Do you get it off when you masturbate?"

Gloria looked at her, blinking. "How many people masturbate?"

"Oh, for Christ's sake," the doctor said. "Everybody does. Everybody. Don't worry about *that*. The question is, does that do it for you?"

"I don't know. I mean, it relaxes me when I'm all full of tension. You know, I can sort of rub on it there and it feels better, a little, and I can go to sleep. But I don't feel like doing that a whole lot. And if I'm really *mad*, nothing helps. But anyway, if *that's* an orgasm, then everybody's doing all this fooling around for nothing. It's just a sort of warm feeling, that's all. I can get *that* just wearing tight Levi's and crossing my legs when I'm sitting down. Get the seam just right. Lord."

Dr. Goldener got up from the desk and went to the window and stood looking out on Park Avenue, her back to Gloria. "I know. Given enough time, tight-fitting jeans can save womankind," she said. "But, no. That is not an orgasm. It isn't bad, mind you, but it's not the real thing. Now. Before we go back to a couple of things you said that particularly interest me, what about your boy friend? Have you tried to make it with another man?"

"Well—uh—just two. But the main one, I thought I would do it with him because he's, well, he's gentle, I guess. Sort of good-looking; a little fattish, maybe, but not bad. But he's not threatening. He's a writer and he's funny and I can control him. You know."

"I know. How has he reacted to all this?"

"Reacted? Mmmm, up to now, he's been patient. Lately, though, he—uh—he has been going through this thing. Well, I mean, he's married and all, and now he thinks he's in love with me. But I can handle all that. What I mean is, he'll still *do*, if I can—"

"All right. You mentioned two. What about the other one?"

Gloria looked up at the ceiling. "*Him*. He's a police—he's a detective. He's all skinny and elbows and ribs and, sure enough, a scrawny little ass, like I thought. And he's got *crispy* hair. It's kind of weird. When he smiles, he looks like a wolf. All smart like that. His eyes always go half closed when he smiles. It's funny how some men can look like that. I mean, look smart when they're really not. He attracts me, too, but in a different way."

"How exactly?"

She considered it, blinking. "Well, Lord, this will make me sound like a real nuthead, Dr.—uh—Goldener. But, well, the way I'm attracted to him is if *he* was the girl and *I* was the man, I'd really *stick* it to him and subdue him and fuck him until he couldn't stand up straight, and cover him with bites. Hard bites, even. Half the time he makes me mad and half the time I feel sorry for him. He's just as dumb as most men and he's working on something he'll never get solved and it's making him go around all red-eyed. More he worries, the better he looks. But it won't work this way and I'll never make it with him because I'm the woman and he's the man and I couldn't control it that way, see?"

The doctor kept her back turned. "I see. It doesn't sound all that nuthead to me, the way you put it. I mean, the way you feel about him, reversing your roles. It sounds like a lot of fun, in fact, and plenty of women feel exactly the same way. It's full of fine psychological undercurrents, but fun anyway. I take it that you tried to ball him as well?"

"Just once so far—and that wasn't much. I was mad at Barry, and Tony and I went out to dinner and some drinks, and then we got up to my place and . . . you know. Oh, we thrashed around a lot and we pretty much got all our clothes off and all. And we kissed a lot; he's a good kisser, but that was it. He started getting all hunchy and he threw one leg up over me and I started to go all upset again. And that was that. I couldn't get as far as I have with Barry, even."

"Too bad." The doctor looked at her watch. "Well, we're just about out of time."

Gloria stood up. "Really? Huh. Damn, I was just about getting to where I was enjoying this. Look, I never talk on and on like this, ever. I mean, tell anybody about how I feel inside. You know."

"I know," Dr. Goldener said. "But that's what I'm here for. Now, there are a couple of things you mentioned earlier that interest me. I want to get right to them next time. One: your reference to somebody getting *to* you. 'Nobody gets to me,' you said. Interesting, that. And two: you referred to times when you were really mad. I take it that you get mad pretty often. I can feel a kind of anger there, bubbling pretty close to the surface at times. And that's perfectly all right; don't worry about it right now. But there is a chance that the one, an outrage over whatever it is, is tied in with the other, the sexual frustration. I don't want this to sound too heavy, kid, but it is possible that if we fix one, we fix the other. Two for the price of one, and at seventy dollars an hour, that's not bad. Anyway, we'll see. But—"

"Don't worry about my temper," Gloria said. "I can control my temper. Always have. If I thought it was a problem, I would have told you. No, I *told* you what the problem was. Not temper."

Dr. Goldener nodded, looking at her. "Sure, sure. But anyway, I want you to think about it during the week, all right? Do it for me. Next time, I want to talk about people or events getting to you. If it proves not to be important, we'll drop it and go on to something else. After all, it's your money."

"Okay, then," Gloria said. "I for sure don't follow you through all this, but okay. See, the thing is . . . I mean, the reason it's such a waste of time, is easy. If an event or a person gets to me, well, I can sure enough take care of that. And I do, too. Just take care of it and get it out of the way. But my problem is, it's my dumb old body here. That's where I need your help. Lord, maybe I'm making too much of it; you know, sex hang-ups and all. But if everybody else can go all the way and get their gun off, then I want it, too. That's the one part I can't take care of all by myself. Everything else, I can."

"Fine. That's better."

"I mean, I can help myself. Understand?"

"I understand."

"If something has to be done, I do it."

"Right."

"So that's not the problem."

Dr. Goldener opened the door. "Whatever you say, Gloria. See you next week. Be a good girl in the meantime."

thirty

HE BLINKED SEVERAL TIMES, sucking in his breath, then took the napkin from his lap and dabbed at his eyes with it. He was still holding the fantail shrimp by the tailpiece. He leaned over and looked into the white bowl. And then he swallowed and looked at Gloria. "What in heaven's name do they put in that sauce?" he said.

"It's some kind of special curry stuff," she said. "You just took too big a dip for a beginner, Mr. Wynn. Boy, you effete Californians, anyway. Now, take a sip of water and start all over again. Next time, you just sort of barely *skim* the shrimp across the top of the sauce. Like this, see? And then later, when you get the inside of your mouth all toughened up, you can just mash the whole shrimp down around in there."

She had taken him to the House of Chan because this was the way that she had decided to get it going. Besides, he had kept insisting that she join him for dinner, and the Americana Hotel, where they were holding his convention, was right across the street. And as long as she had finally decided to go ahead and do it—and as long as he was going to be the one—she had figured that she might as well stock up on fantail shrimp so that the whole thing wouldn't be a loss.

It had been Dr. Goldener's idea. At first Gloria had yelled at her a lot, had even gotten up out of the beige leather chair and stamped all around the office, shouting. But slowly, the doctor had won out.

"You mean, just haul off and *ball* somebody?" Gloria had said.

"Just flat out like that? Are you kidding me? You mean I'm just supposed to grab some guy and say 'Okay, do me on top of my desk' or something like that? Hell, I just can't—"

"Gloria, Gloria," Dr. Goldener had said, "knock off the crap. I don't mean just to do it to anybody and you know that. Don't do that whole song and dance with me. Back off. I don't mean that you have to walk right out of here today and fuck the *cab*driver. Or your *door*man. We're not talking about that and you damn well know it. We're talking about somebody you like and feel warmly toward. Somebody other than Barry Harkner. The problem is that you're so choked up after all the futile attempts with him that you're overreacting every time he gets close to you. And I have *no* idea how Barry Harkner feels about this, except that I can make a psychological bet on it and give you five-to-one odds. Just about the time you finally relax and decide to let him in there, he's going to be so shocked that he won't be able to get it *up*. And if you think you've got problems now, just wait until that happens."

"But who . . ."

Dr. Goldener had gone through it again. "I don't care *who*. I don't care how. Hell, I don't even care if you finish. Just *try* it with someone else, some warm, compassionate person. Somebody understanding. Older, perhaps. And I don't mean that you have to try it over and over; just once will tell us what we need to know. After all, kid, you can't hurt it—your physical exam showed that you are in fine shape, everything in its proper position—and you certainly can't wear it out, now can you? What if you have just built up too high a wall with Barry? What if someone else were to ring your bell the very first time? Look, Gloria, I'm not Masters or whatever the hell the other one's name is—uh —Johnson. I'm just making a suggestion as one woman to another. It will come to that sooner or later anyway on your own. Except that it will take longer if I just sit here and wait for you to figure it out by yourself. Really. Sure enough, one day you would come running in here and yell, 'Guess what?' Are you with me?"

And finally Gloria had nodded. "You're a bad, bad lady," she had said. "I should report you to the medical whatever it is."

"Nonsense," Dr. Goldener had said. "If I read *Cosmopolitan* correctly, and I'm sure I do, half the male analysts in the world are laying their women patients regularly. All in the name of mental health. And charging them for it, of course."

"Well, would you—uh—do it to one of your men patients if you figured that he needed it?"

"My dear," Dr. Goldener had said, "they *all* need it. But let's not get our roles mixed here. I want you to get out and get going. And if you turn out to be successful, which is entirely possible, please don't call me at home to report. I can wait for your next appointment. If it doesn't work, at least you can get a lovely dinner at some nice place and possibly a Broadway show. As an analyst, I do feel that you need this brief encounter to answer our question, but as a woman, I sure as hell think you shouldn't give it away free. I would *insist* on dinner, at least. Now, goodbye."

And now, holding another shrimp pressed down hard in the sauce, Gloria looked at him critically. He would do just fine, and then she would never have to look at him again. First off, he was so beautiful and serene-looking; and second, he smelled just right, like cracked leather. He had long, slender hands and his gold wedding ring was all buffed down by time. She wondered just how he was going to handle it; he was trying now not to look directly at her breasts—kind of sidewise glances whenever he bent forward to pick up his drink. His sales convention was over tomorrow and he would be going back home. If he knew that she had already decided, chances are he could relax just a little bit more and enjoy his dinner. Hell with that.

"I'm going to have to surrender," he said. "Do you want the rest of my shrimp?"

"Absolutely. Whatever you do, don't let the waiter take them away. Really, Mr. Wynn, you're such a softie. These things are good for you."

"Not good for me; good for you," he said. "And I love to watch you eat. You just seize that shrimp and dip it and then shake it a few times to show it who is boss and then bite it right off at the tail. Actually, you should throw the empty tail shells back over your shoulder; the scene would be perfect. There should be a round native drum right about here, right where that next table is, and the sound of surf crashing in from that wall there. And you could be rising from a giant pearl-lined half shell. Wearing something gossamer. The queen of the seas at her dinner."

Gloria nodded. "You like the gossamer part, don't you?"

"Definitely. In fact, I've thought about nothing else since I met you yesterday."

She sat up a little straighter so that he could get a better look at her chest. She wondered if maybe she should shake her shoulders a little bit to get them moving for him. No. That would be too much too soon. Easy, now.

His name was Page Wynn and he was the public relations vice-president of Galaxy; they had a system that would tie in all the country's computers to one big memory bank sunk underground somewhere in Utah. It would store stuff for everybody in its memory cells, or whatever they called them, and all the subscribers would have to do was to push a few buttons to call in all the facts. The sales convention was to get people to sign on for the service. She didn't begin to understand any of it, and she didn't really care, which was making it hard to get the story checked. Her mind kept wandering off to other things.

She looked at him some more, trying to picture his bare chest under the shirt and tie; he looked like somebody who would wear a V-necked undershirt. He would have blue rayon pajamas laid neatly across the foot of his bed in the hotel and his robe would have a paisley pattern. Silkish.

"Tell me about your wife," she said.

He shrugged. "She's never been really well. A truly fragile woman. She would be taking those very same shrimp and cutting them into impossibly small pieces with a knife and fork and then more or less pushing them around the plate without really eating anything. I guess that's why I'm enjoying this dinner so much. You're so—mmmm—vigorous. I have a daughter about your age. But if anything, she's even more wraithlike than her mother. Here. Please eat this last one. I'll draw upon the nourishment of another martini."

She reached over and picked up his glass and held it up to the light, checking the level. She put it back down. "Don't drink any more of these," she said. "I need you tonight and I can't have you getting all woozy on me."

"Ah, hah," he said. "My mind or my body?"

Well, all right, then. What the hell. She shook her shoulders back and forth a little, watching him. "Oh, no you don't. None of that now. You conventioners are all the same; get you into a big city and you want to run wild. You could just go to your room and drop water bombs out the window like everybody else. Why didn't you bring your wife? She could go shopping or something during your meetings."

"She doesn't travel well. Like certain wines."

"What does that mean?"

He was watching her breasts sway. "Pretty much what it implies. Now, then. As for my mind, how are you doing on your story research? We're leaving tomorrow, you know."

"I know. But I'm just about finished. Got the story right here in my purse."

He looked at her over the rim of his glass, then lowered it. "Uh huh. So that's it. You only agreed to have dinner with me so that—"

"Not entirely," she said. "Not entirely."

"—when it was all over you could fold your napkin and put it down on the table in this businesslike way and say, 'Now, about the story.' Ah, Gloria, my pet, you've done an old man in."

She unsnapped her purse and took out the copy and held it against her chest while the waiter took the dishes away. Then she put it down on the tablecloth and smoothed it out with her fingertips. "No, I haven't either. Honest. First things first, that's all. Just a few more things to check in here and then we're through."

He sipped at the drink again. "Ah, well, if you insist. This simply confirms my belief that a public relations man's work is never done." He took out his half-glasses and put them on, looking at her over the top of them. "What are all those red lines on the copy?"

She reached in the purse again and got out a red pencil and showed it to him. "Well, see, this is the way we work at *Time*. First, the writer writes the story. And then it's all typed up on this computerized copy, this stuff here. And then the researcher has to *check* the whole story, like I told you before. Word by word. Everything. We check all the facts and do all the research all over again, right behind the writer. *Hard* facts are something we can look up, using source stuff; libraries, books, or whatever. But if a writer has *alluded* to something, or if he puts in a supposition maybe, or even a rumor, we have to check that, too. And sometimes we find out that it can't be backed up. Maybe it's libelous. And if so, we won't let them keep it in the story. We just flat say, 'You can't say that,' and—"

"Such power for a young girl."

"You bet it is. Anyway, the red-pencil system started years ago; it helps us keep track. I take a story and as I check out everything in it, I put a little red line under that word. It's even become part of the language at *Time* magazine. You know, someone will say something and someone else will say, 'Is that a red check?' Meaning, is it correct? Or 'Are you a red check on that?' You know."

"I'm impressed," he said. "May I read the story?"

"You're not allowed."

"All right, then. Perfectly understandable." He took off the glasses and folded them and slipped them back into his pocket. "You'll have to ask me the questions yourself."

She leaned back in her chair now and looked at him. Absolutely perfect. She could practically *cue* him from here on in and he would respond, coming along obediently like a Greer County coon-dog pup. That's the thing about men—they were so damn shallow. She would tell Dr. Goldener about it, about how she had set it all up and then led him through it. Lord, maybe even the sex would be good. He probably smelled like cracked leather all over. And he sure as hell looked like he could do it well. A lot of old men looked like that, like they had all the moves down pat. And if she could get the lighting in his room just right so that she wouldn't have to look at him much, well . . .

"Question?" he said.

"Oh . . . mmmm." She leaned forward again and turned over a few pages. "Mmmm. Here. The writer compares your computer center to a wartime bunker. He calls it a place chiseled into a Utah mountainside and im . . . impregnable." She picked up the pencil and held it alongside that line in the copy.

"Well, a bit too romantic, I fear. The Galaxy center isn't something out of *Where Eagles Dare*. Putting the computer in Utah wasn't so much a matter of security as it was space, you see. Further, the land is cheaper, as is the labor. No, I would suggest that 'bunker' is an allusion about which you can use your powers as a researcher to protest."

She wrote a tiny NO in the right margin. "All right." She turned over two more pages. "The writer says that—mmmm—let's see. That the computer when fully assembled would be about the size of the main lobby of Grand Central Station."

He frowned, nodding. "Well, that sounds about right to me,

although that's not the comparative image we provided him originally. New York writers tend to lean to New Yorkish images. As I recall, I used something about the size of the Rose Bowl at field level. It's closer to home, for one thing, and it provides more of an image that would be readily recognizable by readers of *Time*, I would think. Ummm, listen . . ."

She smiled at him, waiting. All right, let's go, dummy. Let's shake it here.

"I happen to have all the exact statistics back at the hotel. Measurements, diagrams. Are there any more technical questions in there that need precise checking?"

Way to go, my old man. Ah, dear Lord, if Dr. Goldener could only see her now. This was getting to be sort of real fun, in a way. Hell, if he was half this easy to steer around in bed, maybe he could even . . . well, we'll soon know.

"Yes, indeed there are," she said.

He put his drink down and signaled for the check. "Well, then. If you have a few minutes, we could run over to my room and go over the material. I'll even give you some extra sources for checking. It won't take long. And then perhaps we could have an after-dinner drink."

"All right," she said. "I'd really like to get all this stuff checked out before you leave."

"Fine, fine." He stood up and came around to hold the back of her chair.

"I'll just freshen up a bit," she said. "And I'll meet you at the front door, all right? Be sure to tip the man well."

"Consider it done, my dear. In the best expense-account manner."

In the bathroom, sitting on the toilet seat behind the latched door, she looked down at her underpants pulled to just above her knees. There was a tiny raveled place on the waistband just in front and the pinkish elastic showed through. Maybe she should have worn the Pucci's after all, but she hadn't really counted on getting it this far along when she had been getting dressed. Well, no matter, really. You do it all with lighting anyway, and plain old rayon panties wouldn't matter then. Hell, she could probably sneak them off while he wasn't looking. She tore off some toilet paper, folded it over and then reached under and patted herself dry. She stood, tugging up her pants. Then she bent and pulled up her jeans, zipped up the fly and snapped the waist closed. Time for the big test. She flushed the toilet. If Dr. Goldener was *right*, she was going to march right back over to the office and kick Barry a good one right in the ass. She unlatched the door and went out.

He was waiting for her and took her lightly by the elbow and guided her out the door.

"You smell like cracked leather," she said.

"Cracked?"

"Yes. You sure do. You know, it's like when you go into the equipment room at school; it's usually a big closet, really. And you open the door and step in and suddenly you're surrounded by this great smell of all the beat-up old shoulder pads and kidney protectors. And shin guards for field hockey. They've been used for years and years and they're sitting on the shelves and the leather is all *cracked*, see? It gives off a very special smell and it fills up your whole body."

"I think I follow you," he said. "I'm not sure just how I should react to that. But I think—"

"It's a wonderful smell," she said.

They went through the hotel lobby.

"I'll just get my key," he said.

She waited by the elevators for him.

"There, now. Heaven knows, it isn't much, but it's home," he said. "I have a little wine chilling up there."

"Doesn't everybody?"

"Nightcap," he said. "Remember?"

When they got off on twenty-two, he was resting his arm lightly across her shoulders. They walked down the hall that way. "Here," he said. He stooped and unlocked the door and ushered her inside. The room smelled pretty much the way he did.

But it wasn't pajamas; it was his dressing gown lying neatly across the foot of the bed.

"See?" he said. "Wine, as promised." The ice bucket was sitting on the coffee table; he spun the wine bottle around a few times between the palms of his hands, then picked it up and shook the water off the bottom. "Just absolutely the proper temperature."

She stood still and looked around the room for a moment. Then she walked over and clicked off the floor lamp that was standing behind the wing chair. She backed up a few steps and squinted at it. She stepped over to the nightstand and turned that lamp on, swung her head around to check, then turned it back off. She straightened and went to the bathroom door, reached in and turned on the light and then eased the door almost closed, so that a narrow shaft of light fell diagonally across the foot of the bed and his robe.

He was watching, tugging at the cork. "What in the world are you doing?"

"Fixing all the lights," she said. "There, now. You like it?"

"I *love* it." He paused, almost motionless, looking at her intently. Then he took a deep breath. "And now that you have the lighting fixed up to your satisfaction?"

She shrugged, setting both breasts into the soft sway for him to look at.

He stared at the front of her blouse where the nipples were clearly defined. He put the wine bottle back into the bucket and walked closer. He bent his head to look down at her, then put his hands on her shoulders. His hands were still cold from the wine bottle. "I love it," he said. "And you, my pet."

She got her mouth set just right and tilted her head back.

"Gloria," he said. "Glory. Glory-child. My little girl. Little Glory."

She opened her mouth right away for the kissing, letting him do all the things with his tongue, and she swung her hips forward hard, pressing into him. He brought his hands back from her shoulders, his elbows out, and held the palms of his hands against the sides of her breasts where they were squeezed up tight against his rib cage. The hands were a little warmer now, but not that much.

"Love," he said. His voice had turned husky, just like that. "My little love."

He slid his hands around to her back and then moved them down, until one hand cupped each cheek of her backside. She continued to grind it into him. Then, almost staggering, he began to back slowly toward the bed, still holding her. It was very hard to walk that way. And the cracked-leather cologne was starting to make her eyes water.

The backs of his knees hit the bed and he stopped, wavering slightly backward. She worked her arms loose and got him by the waist gently and lowered him backward into a sitting position. Then she stood up.

He leaned forward, putting his arms around her hips, and buried his face in her stomach, his chin just at her waist and the top snap of her jeans. Then he pulled one hand back around to the front and tugged at the snap until it came open. And he nuzzled his face inward, turning it back and forth against her shirt until he could kiss her on the bare stomach. She got a handful of his hair and eased his head back, looking down at him.

"Wait," she said.

She stepped back a few steps, looking around the room. The line of light from the bathroom door fell across his shoulders. She nodded at him and began to unbutton her shirt, tugging it up out of her jeans.

He leaned forward again, his arms out. "Glo—"

She shook her head no. Then she walked around to the other side of the bed, so that the shaft of light was directly at her back. She shifted from side to side until, when she stood with her legs apart, the light came right through there. She unzipped the jeans and pulled them down; when she was bent over like that, the light came up across her shoulders and fell full on his face so that she could watch him. She stood up again to step out of the jeans, throwing him back into full shadow. She put both thumbs under the waistband of her panties, hiding the raveled part with the palms of her hands, and then eased them down, bending over again, watching him.

He was frozen into place.

She stood on one leg, shaking the underpants off the toes of her right foot.

"Now, then," she said. "Take your clothes off."

He blinked into the beam of light shining out from between her legs. He moved his mouth a few times, but nothing came out.

"Come on," she said.

She watched while he stood and began to fumble with his pants, her hands on her hips, her legs apart.

Time to win one for Dr. Goldener.

"Hurry it up," she said. "Let's go."

thirty-one

HE RAISED UP on one elbow, the shock of gray hair all messed down across his forehead, and looked at her. "More wine? Or more anything?"

"More wine," Gloria said. "Just wine."

She had the bathroom water glass balanced on her bare stomach, holding it lightly with her fingertips. He reached across and got the bottle from the nightstand and poured some wine into the glass.

"Don't worry. If I spill any on your lovely little tummy, I can always kiss it off," he said.

"You've already done all that," she said.

She looked up at the ceiling, letting her breathing get back into the normal range, thinking about it.

Christ on a *crutch*. About the only thing that she felt right now was *used*. Well, used and wet, with stuff seeping out. If she had been reading all those things correctly, the magazine articles and all, Page was what they would call an accomplished lover. Great staying power that was supposed to be so important; he had lasted and lasted. And he had tried all sorts of trick things, too, some gymnastic maneuvers with a tangle of arms and legs, and there had been a couple of times in the heavy going there when she thought that she might have to give him respiration or something. And finally, he had fallen face down across her legs, his arms hanging down over the side of the bed.

But zero. Absolute zero.

Now he held the cigarette over to her mouth so that she could take a drag. "Are you happy?"

"Yeah. Delirious."

"I'm glad." He sprawled over on his back again. "You have certainly made me very happy."

"I'm glad."

"I mean, I wanted to make love to you from the very first moment that you sought me out downstairs and introduced yourself," he said. "What man wouldn't? You were magnificent then, magnificent. That tumbling wild mane of blond hair. The splendid body, all long-legged and businesslike. Heads turned all across the exhibition hall when you passed. I watched them. I was hopelessly stricken from the start, from the moment we met. Under your spell. Are you aware that you cast spells?"

"I don't know about casting them. But I sure got one hanging over me."

He ran the tips of his fingers lightly down the top of her left thigh, raising a trail of goose pimples and making the little hairs stand up behind it. "A good spell, of course."

"Sure."

He pressed a little harder with the fingertips, then slid his hand around to cup the inside of her thigh. "Would you like to . . ."

Gloria shook her head, looking at the ceiling. "No. About one more time around like that, Page, and you're going to split a kidney or something."

"I'll go slower this time."

"No. And take your hand away from there."

"Can you stay for the night? Perhaps in the morning, after some sleep, we can—"

"No. Your *hand*, Page."

"All right." He lay back again. "I understand. But you have still made me very happy. Happiest man in all the Americana Hotel on this very night. All up and down this hotel, on all the floors, there are unhappy men. Watching Johnny Carson or whatever. Drinking warm Black Label out of bathroom glasses, their vision growing dim. But not me. Glory?"

"Hmmm?"

"How old are you?"

"Twenty."

"And liberated."

She turned her head to look at him. "Careful how you use that word."

"No, no. Please don't misunderstand. No, I mean wonderfully liberated. Totally, in its purest sense. Free of all the stuffy inhibitions that are shot all through my generation. Young, Gloria, young. I love it, and I envy you. *That's* what I mean by liberated. Your generation has managed to erase all the pretenses that mine hasn't. You see?" He got up on one elbow again, looking down at her. "You're free to say yes, free to say no, as the spirit moves you. No role playing. No elaborate mating dance. By that I mean where a man and a woman circle each other warily, volleying back and forth all the introductory phrases that lead to the simple act of going to bed. Right?"

"Mmmm."

"No, really. Look, you came up to me in the exhibit hall. Young, forthright. Wearing blue jeans, for heaven's sake. Blue *jeans*. And—"

"They cost fifty dollars a pair, Page."

"No. It's the *image*, my dear. The freeness of it. It's you and your generation. That's what I'm saying. Ah, dear God, to be that way. And then. And then, when you decided to take me to bed, why—you just *did* it. I had hoped; no, I had half-hoped, to seduce you. I ordered this wine before we went to dinner, embarrassing myself with my own plans. I put the ice bucket there, on the coffee table. Then I moved it to the nightstand. No, that would be too obvious. So I moved it again. How ancient of me; how unnecessary. I laid out my robe. Pajamas, too, but then I put them away again. And all the while I was afraid of the one thought going through me. It was the fear that you might laugh at me. Laugh? No, a mere curl of your lip would have done it. But then you simply came right up here, adjusted all the lights and pulled off your clothes. And we made love. Made it and *made* it. Now, it might not have been enough for you on *my* part, but I may never be that good again. It marked my finest hour. What you probably demand, I mean, with that fantastic sensuality of yours, is two people. I mean, two *men* at once, at the same time, both paying homage to your young superbody. But if that's not to be, well, I love what we've had."

She wriggled her toes, bending her head forward and sighting down between her breasts at them. She really had to go to the bathroom. "You're very sweet," she said. "You're a good man."

"You sure you don't want us to—"

"No, Page. I *said*."

He nodded. "I even love that frankness about you. It's just exactly right."

"Thank you."

"I can speak as frankly to you, can't I?"

"Yes, Page. I have to get up here in a minute."

"I mean, frank in the sense that I can tell you what I have in mind?"

"Ummm hmmm, yes."

He reached over with his hand and drew a circle with his fingertip all around her belly button. "The two men . . . Well, I spoke earlier about two men at once. I don't think you were listening; you didn't react. But it's the ultimate in erotic experiences. The end of the *world*. You people . . . No, let me reword that. Your generation, your free spirits, openly sensual; you do it all the time. We see it in movies and we hear constant allusions to it and . . . you know. We go weak with envy. And—"

She moved his finger aside, holding it lightly in her hand. "Don't do that," she said. "I have to go to the bathroom."

"And I wonder if—"

"If what?"

He moved her hand aside and bent forward, rubbing the tip of his chin lightly down the centerline of her stomach. He paused at the belly button and kissed it. And then he licked it with his tongue, moving it in widening circles. He stopped and spoke without raising his head and his voice sounded muffled.

"I wonder if you would consider something. Speaking frankly, as I just said. The president of our company is just down the hall on this floor. A wonderful man, full of life. Like us. You'd love him on sight. A nice guy. And he would certainly love you, no question about that. If I called him, he could be over here in a flash. And the—uh—the three of us could—"

"Could what?"

He swung his head around and looked up at her. "The three of us could make love. All at once. You know, two men at the same time, both doing their very best to make you happy. Possibly ecstatic. It would certainly make *us* happy; he and I have done this before and, I assure you, it's marvelous. We would treat you very tenderly. And if it's a matter of financial consideration, well . . ."

She raised up on her elbows and looked down at him. "Get

your head away from down there," she said. "Come on, up. Up. Did I just hear you right?"

He nodded. "Yes."

"Two men at once? You mean one man at this end and one man at that end down there?"

He smiled, blinking.

"Page, are you crazy or something? Stop grinning at me like that. Are you kinky or what?"

"It isn't kinky," he said. "It's delightful. Remember the old adage about two heads are better—"

"Page, stop doing all that, I said. You're getting my stomach all wet doing that. Come on. Your *president?*"

"He's just down the hall."

"You mean, call him on over here and . . ."

He nodded again.

"Page, are you serious? Come on. That's about the kinkiest dumb thing I ever heard and . . . uhhh. Come on. You're kidding me, aren't you?"

He looked into her eyes for a long moment. Then he sighed. "Yes," he said. "I'm just kidding you. I'm sorry. I didn't mean that you should take me seriously. An old man's joke. I—uh—I just thought it would amuse you, the imagery there. The president *is* just down the hall, but I—"

"God, if I thought for one minute that you—"

"No. No, don't get upset. I was just—mmmm—just talking. You know, saying things that came into my head. A little joke."

She plopped back down on the pillows again and looked at the ceiling. "All right. Forget it. Some folks sure have a weird sense of humor, is all."

He swung his legs around and got off the bed and walked over to the dresser. From the back, his buttocks looked droopy and scrawny. "I'm sorry about that. I thought you would find it amusing. But, anyway, on to more important things. I'll want your address and telephone number."

"Why?"

He came back carrying a little notebook and a gold ball-point pen and sat down on the side of the bed. "Well, I'll want to see you again, needless to say. I'll be coming back to New York from time to time. I'll always call ahead, naturally. But in a company the size of *ours*, with all our sales contacts, well . . . Now then, what's the number?"

"Why?"

He smiled at her. "Why? Why, fantail *shrimp*, that's why. To coin a phrase, that is. Fantail shrimp dinners. Night spots, perhaps. Discos, I believe it is. Dancing in your fifty-dollar jeans. What is it that your crowd always says? Ummm, you dig it? The very spirit of liberated New York. And . . . Now don't look at me like that. I have already explained what I mean about liberated."

She sat up on the bed and pulled up her legs and put her arms around them. Her head was starting to hurt now. The light from the bathroom door was tracing a narrow path right across the top of his head, turning the gray hair into pure shine, like chrome.

"What did you say?" she said.

"I am merely suggesting modestly that I know everybody in the world. Fantail shrimp lovers among them. Admirers—no, lovers—of willowy girls in faded blue jeans. Such is the lot of vice-presidents in charge of public relations. It *falls* to public relations vice-presidents to know everybody in the world, doesn't it? And if I *may*, I would like to be able to respond should someone ask me if I know anybody in New York, that yes, indeed, I know the most perfectly marvelous young thing. Gloria. The lovely Glory."

She looked at him, blinking. Then she folded her arms over her breasts and hugged hard. "Oh, God," she said. "Oh, God."

"And they can phone you and— Gloria? Is something wrong?"

She scooted back on the bed until she bumped into the headboard. The Naugahyde was cold across her shoulders.

"Page," she said, "I got to get out of here."

"Whatever for? Please don't leave me now. My *dear*. For one moment there, you looked alarmed. Certainly not by me, I hope. Now then, where was I? Ahhh, yes. Your telephone number. Now, if you'll—"

"Page," she said, "stop it. Please."

"I don't understand."

"Page. *You* don't understand—don't understand what you're *doing* to me. Christ, you were *serious* about the other thing, too; you and your president. You weren't joking, like you said. Two men at once and all that ecstasy crap. That's *dirty*. And financial consideration, you said. I guess it didn't sink in at first. But now—"

"No. No, it was a little joke, I promise. In poor taste, now that I look back on it."

She uncoiled her legs and got off the other side of the bed. Then she leaned forward and put both hands down on it, shaking her head and looking at him. "Page, please. Is that what public relations vice-presidents do? They fix up computer customers with girls? Or the *president?* With dates? Is that what they do? They open that little book there in your hand and they say, 'I've got a hot number in Manhattan. You just have to buy her a few fantail shrimp.' Is that it? Please, Page. Say no."

He closed the book and tossed it on the nightstand, then leaned over and put the ball-point pen on top of it. "But, Glory, dear, I'm trying to *help*. And you, more than anybody, I would think, would understand. You're that *free*, as I have said. No. Let me use another word. You're of this new, *aware* generation. And you—"

She shook her head back and forth, biting hard at her lower lip. "No, Page. Don't say the rest of it."

He sat up a little straighter and stiffened his shoulders. "Well, I certainly *shall* say it. I'll say it because I admire it so, as I told you. You're free, and you're aware. And, remember, you are the one who made it clear to *me*. You came up here all young and alive, exercising your own spirit. It was your choice. Of all people, you should be the last one to be offended by—"

"Oh, Christ. There are other names in that book?"

He shrugged just a bit. "Well, there are other names in there, yes. Of course there are. One makes contacts. But by that you shouldn't draw the inference that—"

"But names. Girls. Their phone numbers."

"I thought you understood that, Gloria. I don't understand you. Why are you so upset? Now, we had a wonderful time together, didn't we? We did. And, in fact, you reaffirmed my faith in youth, you really did. Now, for my part, I can return the favor by—"

She stood up straight and took several quick breaths. "Page, stop it! Stop all of it. There's a name for what you are. A *name* for it. Men who sell women's services. Bodies, their telephone numbers. It doesn't have to be money. It doesn't matter whether you're operating down there on the *street* or not, Page. Just buy one of our computers and I'll get you laid. Jesus, Page. You're nothing but a fucking—"

He held up one hand, the palm toward her. "*Hold* it! Wait. I am nothing of the kind. Public relations men are— Look, I am not *selling* you. Good heavens. I thought that you would appreciate this. Your phone number. A friendly call while one is in New York on business. Perhaps dinner. Nothing more, nothing less; it would all be up to *you*, Gloria. You could still do what you wanted. Well, I can see that you don't understand my role in all of this. I can *see* that I was wrong to think that you would. I thought you would love the idea."

"Pimp," she said.

He stiffened his shoulders again. "*What* did you call me? That's ridiculous. Obscene. I think you had better go now." He raised one arm and pointed at her. "You had better leave this room immediately."

She walked around the bed toward the pile of her clothes on the floor. She raised one foot and kicked the panties out of the way, then bent down and picked up the jeans. She held them by the waist with her left hand and began reaching into the right front pocket. "Too late," she said. "Not now. Not yet."

He stood and walked over close to her, thrusting out his chin. "I said you'll have to leave."

She shook her head no. "Pimp Page. Page Pimp. You pimping son of a bitch."

He drew back his left arm, the hand open. "Don't *say* that. Don't *ever*. I'm in public relations. You say something foul like that one more time and I'll have to slap you."

She looked into his eyes. "Pimp," she said.

And as he swung his arm around, she lifted her right hand out of the jeans pocket and rolled her hand over to open the blade.

thirty-two

SHE GOT THE TAPE RECORDER from Nancy's top right-hand drawer and carried it into the front room and put it down on the coffee table beside the wineglass. Then she sat down on the floor and leaned over and checked it. The fat side of the tape was showing on the left through the little window; the battery was reading fine. She reached up with her right hand and punched down the Record and Forward switches and looked into the little window again to make sure that the sprockets were turning. She cleared her throat. It was 2:10 A.M.

"Dear Nancy," she said.

She reached across and picked up the wineglass, spilling a trail of burgundy across the tabletop and on across her knee. She took a sip and held it in her mouth for a moment, then swallowed.

"Nancy, this is Stormy," she said. "I came home and you weren't here. And when you come home, I won't be here. There'll just be this dumb tape; I'll be long gone. Some of my *stuff* will be here. A whole lot of my stuff. You can take it all out and put it in a big pile in the middle of the floor here and you can give it all away at your next feminist discussion group, all right? Whatever fits anybody, I don't care. What you can't give away, go ahead and throw away. I don't care. None of the stuff will fit you because you're too goddamn fat anyway. You're a goddamn fat slob, Nancy Marie; always have been. I . . . no."

She took another sip of the wine, thinking, squinting at the turning sprockets through the little window.

"No. Go back and erase that first part there. I'd do it myself, but I don't know how. All right. Now. *Dear Nancy*. Nancy, I flat can't stand it and I'm gone. Okay? I only said that first part about fat because I'm so goddamn mad. It's ass-kicking time, like we used to say back home. You remember that? Your daddy said it; mine, too. Nothing's right around here and it's *justice* time. Everybody waits; nobody makes the first move. Nobody. Things are flat wrong out there. Lord, people are hurting each other so bad. Well, shit, oh, dear. Somebody had to make the first move. You understand that part, don't you? Oh, sure. Sure, you-all sit around here and talk it up real big. Equality for women. And while you're doing that, they're down *there*, down outside there, hauling and kicking women all around. God. Little, teeny young girls with frizzy hair. Icky, dumb-ass girls. But who is to help them? At train stations; no, bus depots, I mean. "Somebody din' meet you, sugah?' My God. It's bad, really bad. And Janie, sitting there on the subway. Man just ups and whips it out and sticks it toward her *face*. I don't know, Nancy. Did I tell you about the man in the park? Yes, I remember I told you. Did anybody help me? No. Did anybody move to help Janie? Well, I'll tell you what: they *never* will. Not here; not anywhere, I guess. It was me, I'd have leaned over and *bit it off* if there wasn't anything else I could get my hands on right then. I know I'd have done *some*thing. Nobody does *me* that way. No-body. But it isn't just me; it's everybody should strike back. Just flat do it. New York *City* won't care. One: they won't care, which counts for a lot. And two: it's too big a city and it loses you. You could do anything and they'd never catch up to you anyway. But I guess mostly it's a matter of don't-caring. You just got to do it all yourself. Oh, I know, I know. 'Vengeance is mine . . . saith the Lord.' I don't know what made me think of that just now, but there you go. It flat doesn't *work*, Nancy. If you need vengeance, if you got to have some right *now*, where is the Lord? Hell, I don't know; He's over on the other side of town somewhere. Delivering babies or something. Anyway, it takes too long to wait, while all the bad stuff, the really pukey stuff, just goes on and on and on. And you're all so tender-hearted that . . . it's just that the city makes you-all too scared. Nobody . . ."

She reached for the wine again and knocked the glass over on its side. She watched it spread out for a moment, then swiped at it with her forearm, rubbing in circles, soaking it up with her shirt sleeve. She bent her arm back and looked at it, nodding. Then she turned back to the tape recorder.

"And, well, all right. *Dear Nancy.* I'm going away for good. Don't know where. But I went and took all my money and I took the wine money, too. Call my folks, don't call them; I don't give a shit. Save my name tag off my office. I may want it sometime. Just stick it away in a drawer someplace. Tell everybody goodbye, I guess. And"—she leaned forward again and checked the tape—"give all my Pucci underwear to Barry. Not to *wear;* he can put it under his pillow or something. Hang it off one ear, all I care. Poor, fat old bugger. Wouldn't have worked anyway, with Barry. Dr. Goldener said. Huh. And I still owe her seventy dollars from last time. But the way things worked out, she ought to pay *me* the seventy. So we're all even; you tell Dr. Goldener that for me. She won't understand, but tell her anyway. Or don't tell. I don't care anymore. She didn't help. You didn't help me. Nobody helped. I had to do everything myself. Well . . ."

The tape was almost gone. She took a deep breath and raised her voice a bit.

"Dear Nancy. So long."

thirty-three

THE DOORMAN LOOKED BOTH WAYS on the street, hunching his shoulders against the rain, then came back in through the swinging door. "Hardly ever any cabs this time of night, Mizz Cooper," he said. "And with this rain and all, they all go hide someplace."

"That's all right," Gloria said. "I'll just wait."

She put down the small bag, stood up and put both hands in her raincoat pockets. Then she walked over to the door and leaned her forehead against the glass, soaking up the cold, and looked out. Just at the outer edge of the short awning, the water was coming in slantwise with the wind, bouncing high enough to make the sidewalk go all fuzzy and hard to see.

"Awful time of night to have to go somewheres," he said.

"I know."

"Where—uh . . . How far do you have to go, Mizz Cooper?"

Gloria kept her head against the glass, watching the rain. "Long, long ways."

"Well, look, I gotta go and check on—"

"It's all right," she said. "Go on ahead and do what you have to do. First cab comes along, I'll just run out and catch it. Go ahead."

"Thank you, ma'am."

She listened to his footsteps shuffling away, fading out. Both her hands were steady now, and in her right coat pocket, the curve of the razor fit warmly into the fold between her four fingers and her palm. She rubbed her thumb back and forth against the smoothness of the pearl handle, polishing it.

The car came down the street, sending out little, surflike waves from the front tires, and stopped, double-parked, in front of the hotel across the way. It sat there, windshield wipers swinging, the rain sluicing off the roof and down the sides. It was a Lincoln with whitewall tires. The sheets of water made the windows all opaque.

She straightened up, watching, then wiped her forehead with her left coat sleeve.

A man got out of the car and ran toward the hotel, taking high, dainty steps in the rain. He went up the stairs and in through the door.

She put her forehead back against the window.

About three minutes went by, the Lincoln just sitting there with its wipers going. And then the man came out again, the collar of his coat turned up. It was a long coat, fitted in tightly at the waist, with a belt that tied so that both long ends hung down. He high-stepped back to the car and bent down out of sight for a moment, opening the door. Then the top of his head appeared and he backed away a few steps, nodding and seeming to say something. Another head showed up—a girl in a ski parka. She was wearing a knapsack sort of shoulder bag. She turned back to the car for a moment, then stood up again, holding a scarf up over her head, both elbows out. The man took her gently by the front of the parka and tugged.

Gloria straightened again, squinting into the rain.

An empty cab came along slowly, swinging around the double-parked Lincoln, spray coming up from the front tires.

She lifted her hands out of her coat pockets and put her palms against the door glass, pushing, then stopped. She let the door hiss closed again. She watched the cab go out of sight and then turned her head back to look at the man and the girl.

The man had both arms out now, the palms up, and she could see his mouth moving. The girl was facing him, shaking her head no under the scarf. The girl turned her head back and forth in a steady rhythm.

The man stamped one foot, then lifted it up and looked at his pants leg. Then he reached over and got the front of the girl's parka again and pulled it toward him. The girl leaned back.

Gloria put both hands back in her coat pockets.

The man leaned forward and seemed to knock on the window of the Lincoln, then straightened and waved it away; long, sweeping waves with one hand. The car eased out slowly, leaving the two people standing alone on the sidewalk.

The man still had the girl by the front of her parka. She was still shaking her head no under the scarf. And now, suddenly, he swung his other hand around hard and slapped her with the open palm. And bringing it back, putting more shoulder into it, he slapped her again the other way, with his knuckles. The force of the slaps sent an arc of spray off her cheeks, making a quick, fuzzy halo around her shoulders. She sagged a bit, leaning forward, and he pushed her back upright. He grabbed at her scarf and threw it down on the sidewalk.

Gloria took two quick breaths, moving her thumb back and forth again along the smooth pearl panel inside her right hand.

The man across the street got the girl by one arm and turned, leading the way to the hotel steps, pulling hard. At the bottom of the steps he yanked her around in front of him, then pushed her up with both hands at her back. They went in through the door and it swung closed behind them.

Gloria watched for a few minutes more, breathing through her mouth.

Another empty cab came by and the driver braked it a bit just outside the awning, squinting out through his window at her.

Gloria shook her head no; the driver shrugged and the cab pulled away.

Then she turned up her coat collar and pushed the glass door open. She walked out under the awning, looking at the hotel door across the street.

And then, jamming her hands back in her coat pockets, she tightened her shoulders and sprinted across the street, up the stairs and into the hotel.

thirty-four

THE SERGEANT WATCHED the Lincoln pull away. He was holding the umbrella so low that the inside ribs pressed down on the top of his head. But still the spray came in and he could sense the water running off the front of his coat. Both feet were soaked now, cold, and he moved his toes up and down inside his shoes. He watched the man and the girl in the parka, both of them left standing on the sidewalk in front of the hotel. He needed a cigarette. It was 2:50 A.M.

The couple was arguing now, the girl shaking her head back and forth steadily. She was holding something up over her head, a scarf or something.

"Station One?"

He brought his left arm up and held the mobile unit diagonally at the side of his face, then pressed down the transmitting switch with his thumb. "Station One," he said. "Go ahead."

The voice came back slightly cracked. "Station Two here. How you holding up, sergeant?"

He pressed on the switch again. "I'm wet. And cold. Where are you?"

"I'm in the car. Across the street; behind you and to your left, where you wanted. You ready to be relieved? Over."

He swung his head back to check the man and the girl again. The man was tugging at the front of her parka.

"Maybe in a minute, all right?"

"Any time you say. Wait. Just a sec. I'm getting another call here on the car radio. Get right back to you."

The sergeant moved his arm back down, watching the man and the girl. Now the man swung his free arm around and slapped her hard, first this way, then once coming back. The spray flew off the girl's face.

"God*damn*," the sergeant said.

The man pulled the girl over to the steps, then switched around and pushed at her. They went in through the door, out of sight.

"Station One?"

He raised the unit again and pushed down the switch. "Go ahead. Station One here."

"DeMario?"

"Yes. Go ahead."

"We just got another one. Desk just called me. You read me?"

"Another one what?"

"Slasher. Americana Hotel. Worst one yet, he said."

He looked down the empty street. "A *pimp?* At the Americana? Over."

"I don't know, a pimp. But slashed all to hell. All they said was it was an old guy. Executive of something, some computer company or something like that. But he's spread all over the place up there. Throat cut down to his backbone. Sliced right up the middle; all hacked out at the crotch. The same M.O. Over."

The movement at the door under the awning caught his eye and the sergeant swung his head around as she came out. She stood under the awning, looking across the street at the hotel where the man and the girl had just gone in.

"DeMario?"

The sergeant punched down the switch again with this thumb. "Hold it," he said.

"But I was saying. This guy at the Americana. All cut—"

"Hold it, *hold* it. Everybody stand by."

He eased the switch up, poised, holding the mobile unit about three inches from the side of his face. He watched her.

She jammed her hands down in her raincoat pockets and thrust her shoulders forward.

"*No*," the sergeant said, squinting at her. "No, Gloria, NO. Goddamn it, *don't*. Go on back in*side*. Go away, for Christ's sake. Just don't do this. Come on. Please."

She lowered her head and ran out from under the awning, almost in a sprint, her feet kicking up big splashes when they hit the street. She ran up the steps and into the hotel.

"Awww, *shit*," he said. Then he pressed down on the switch with his thumb again and spoke into the unit. "All *right*. Station One. Everybody in. Everybody. Come on, you bastards. *Move* it."

The voices began crackling back. "Station Two. Right here." And: "Ready on the roof." And: "We're coming in from the corner, sergeant." And: "All set out in back. We're going in now."

He lowered the mobile unit, clicking it off, and stuffed it back in his raincoat pocket. Then he began walking toward the hotel.

Olsen came splashing across the street, holding his gun in one hand, and fell into step alongside.

Up ahead, taking shape fuzzily through the rain, they could see the other officers coming in, moving fast toward the hotel steps.

"Right," Olsen said, panting a bit. "You were right all along."

The sergeant kept walking, feeling the water in his shoes. He threw down the umbrella and kicked at it, bouncing it away into the street. When he spoke, he didn't turn his head to look at Olsen.

"You goddamn dummy, Gloria," he said. "Why you? *Why?* Damn you, you could have gone home. You could have taken your fucking razor and gotten to hell out of my town. My life."

Olsen took the hotel steps two at a time, then paused to turn at the top. He looked down at the sergeant. The water was dripping off the end of Olsen's gun barrel.

"Come on, DeMario," he said. "We don't want to be too late."

The sergeant stood at the foot of the stairs, shoulders hunched up, both hands jammed deep in his pockets. He could feel the rain coming in under his shirt collar now, running in a cold pattern down through the hair on his chest.

"Go ahead," he said. "Get your ass in there. *Move* it. You know what to do."

Olsen swung around and went in the door.

The sergeant looked around at the empty street, then turned and sat down on the second step, sending out an eddy of water on each side. He hung his head down, looking at his feet.

"Too late," he said. "Christ, we were too late the day she came to town."

And then he raised his head again and squinted out into the
street, at the awning across the way. With the rain this way,
pounding in so cold and thick, it was hard to see. Of course, the
tears didn't help any.